AMAZING WONDERS AND MYSTERIES OF THE WORLD

The Three Doctrines in the Kingdom of God

Kabona Nsimbi Bagonza
THE WRITER ON WHOM THE MESSAGE DESCENDED

Joshua Mukalazi   Kizito
WRITER WHO RESEARCHED AND DID THE BOOK

CONTENTS

INTRODUCTION

Praise God the Almighty
Magnify His Name
Glory be to His Holy Name
All nations of the world should praise him.
People of all nations, races and languages in the world should praise
Him forever generation after generation.
The wonders of his work display the firmament.
ALMIGHTY GOD MANIFEST YOURSELF

We are not angels. We are normal human beings. However, we are servants of God and through His Holy Spirit; we are sent to bring the message of God to the people about his judgment because God saw how sinful the world was. This is my duty and service.

With my colleague Joshua Mukalazi Kizito we are sowing the Mustard seed so that it bears fruits because God is not pleased with the way people are ignoring and violating His name deliberately and there after they cry out to Him for help when they get problems. We are God's messengers.

As for me, Kabona Nsimbi Bagonza; Kabona - Literary means to get God's revelation and receiver of God's message and Bagonza means to pacify the sinful nature of the evil world. This means I receive the message of God and if the message is given to the people and it is followed, it helps to pacify the sinful world. It is for this reason that I was given these names. My duty is to give God's message to the people as they pre-pare for God's judgment. God's message is to help people in the world to purify themselves and follow God's ways or turn to him. I have done this duty. The ball is now in your hands to do your part. The work of God is for everybody in the world and not for individuals like me. It has been a noble duty of delivering God's message to the world to help straighten many myths and wrong interpretations about this message. We thank the Almighty God for giving us this opportunity. It is our prayer that even the generations to come will do the right things following our advice. The message in this book has no alterations and it is not exaggerated. It is given as it descended from God to me. Thank You

KABONA NSIMBI BAGONZA
THE WRITER ON WHOM THE MESSAGE DESCENDED

PREFACE

This book is authored by Kabona Nsimbi Bagonza and me, Joshua Mukalazi Kizito. My duty also has been to prepare and publish this manuscript after thorough research and findings about the message of the other author. I have done this research and publication of this book basing on the wealth of experience from my service to the United Kingdom and Buganda Kingdom in various capacities.

We have been doing this in phases and this is the second phase. In the first phase, we wrote about the spiritual world and we indicated that it is real and operational. It was a wide topic, amazing and full of mysteries. Our work in this phase led to the publication of a book entitled "The Discovery of the Hidden Truths and Treasures" meaning Amazima Agaakwekebwa Ensi Gazuuse in Luganda. In this book we tried to indicate the relationship between the spiritual world, the people and God. Therefore after thorough research we have embarked on this second phase.

People of other races in other parts of the world due to rapid civilization and technology, had their heritage values and norms properly documented and properly written in manuscripts or books. We have discovered that our fore fathers of the Black Race did not do this because of unexplainable reasons. However, what they did was that they had these documented in form of riddles, cultural norms and values. These are many and can be explained or elaborated in a wider perspective and subject to different interpretations. Under normal circumstances, Akaalo ka Buganda (The Sacred Cultural Village or the Sanctuary of God) is something that is viewed in terms of a Museum and a tourist attraction. Even the rhyme "Akaalo ka Buganda ka dda" does not bring out its meaning in an elaborate way. However, Akaalo ka Buganda is our heritage that has resulted into the publication of this book. And what is amazing is that, the heritages in this traditional ritual village relate to the entire world and among all nations, races and languages. That is why the facts in this book will leave the reader in wonderment.

When we sin and disobey, God punishes us through His stewards or servants or agents. However, sometimes He uses other methods to put us in order so that we do His will and He forgives us. Therefore, the importance in the sacred cultural village called Akaalo ka Buganda is the link between us and God as we seek for compassion and mercy. This is in addition to God's messengers who are sent from time to time to remind us about God's ways. God's trinity is derived from this.

God's conundrum is intended to give us knowledge. Out of this knowledge we are able to carry out research or studies. From the research we are able to come up with findings or observations and from these we are able to discover the wonders of His creation that displays the firmament. This then gives us more reason to always praise and glorify Him. The discoveries of great men and scientists such as Isaac Newton, Einstein, Vasco Da Gama and many others are practical and display a lot of skill. However, God's spirit and enablement is the science that supported them to achieve this. The spirit is the origination of the science of discovery because He is the beginning, the present and the end of God's covenant in the world.

God is a spirit and guides the Holy Spirit to do His will. The spirit lives in God, in Trinity. The Spirit is part of God's disposition. The spirit is life. The spirit is the guardian; the power and faith. The spirit is a covenant between God and whatever dwells in the Universe and in this covenant God himself is witness. The Holy Spirit is a department of God from which we derive leadership and other aspects.

Therefore depending on my research and findings in the different parts of the world, I have discovered that some people guided by God's Holy Spirit have no opportunity of sending God's message to the world. Many have this to say, "The World was created in phases and God's power manifests itself in different ways to different people of different areas. God works differently to people in different areas depending on their needs and His will. However, as the conquerors or settlers moved to different parts of the world with different interpretations that were not indigenous and that contradict with the heritage of those places have as a result they interfered with God's arrangement for those places."

As a result, many nations are riddled with never ending problems be-cause of assimilating other people's ways of life or cultures that were not adopted for them by God. Every nation has got its ways, uniqueness and destiny. I have also noticed that, it is very important to follow the right path indicated in this book as every race has got its destiny, identity and uniqueness according to God's plan.

I will be very grateful if I see people having the right practices that respect God's plan for mankind. This will save us from wars, natural calamities like floods, famine, earthquakes, diseases, drought, breakdown of society and so forth.

People's morals have greatly degenerated. There is never ending bickering or foul play or dirty politicking among us and everything now is at standstill, with failures in the health systems, with so many wars among us, there is famine and hunger everywhere, with worsening conduct in almost all nations of the world and with our failure to put things back into order. There is anarchy and chaos everywhere. This means that human understanding has come to an end. Then the question is posed. "What should we do to bring back sanity?" The answer is the need to go back to God's arrangements to achieve liberation and freedom. The truth is that we need to go rediscover our cultural values and norms.

JOSHUA MUKALAZI KIZITO

THE WRITER THAT RESEARCHED AND DID THE BOOK

JOSHUA MUKALAZI KIZITO

THE WRITER THAT RESEARCHED AND DID THE BOOK

1
THE TWO ANCIENT KINGS OF BUGANDA
BEMBA-MUSOTA AND KATO KINTU

Since time immemorial, Buganda has been a land of wonders and mysteries because God had made her His sacred sanctuary and home base be-cause of His great grand plan for mankind in the beginning. This sacred sanctuary was rejuvenated during the reign of His Majesty Kato Kintu I. But before this period of His Majesty Kato Kintu I and the subsequent Kings that followed, God administered Buganda directly with the help of His angels and spirits. This period was referred to by the natives as, "Ttonda" a name which literary means Creator. In the "Ttonda" period Adam and Eve also existed in their entities as birth parents from which the White race descends from. This was the same thing for the Bachwezi the Yellow race, the Red race and the Aliens (Abamenke) the Green race. The black races descend from Kintu Kitaka Nawansi Kyawadda but commonly referred to as Kintu or "Kintu kya Beene" which means "God's sacred possession or something that belongs to God" because of the great love that God had towards that possession. Because we became sequential sinners, God used exclusivity as a mark of dissatisfaction so that we relent more and struggle to reach Him. His angels and messengers took dislike towards us, though God bestowed duty upon them to guide us.

When mankind sinned against God, God decreed to let mankind to administer itself but with the guidance of His angels or spirits. He also gave the angels or His spirits leeway to punish mankind particularly whoever departed from God's ways. As the populations grew among the different races, lineages from these different races started to form Nations and were given an opportunity of being independent, with each of these groups forming a state or settlement and a way of life. However, the Baganda maintained the traditions and administrative systems of Kintu Kitaka Nawansi Kyawadda the forefather of the Black race.

The period of Ttonda was followed by that of Muwawa. The world was vast in its emptiness and not only physically but also in ideology or thought and therefore referred to as Muwawa despite the formation of nations. The first King in this Muwawa period in Buganda was Muwawa Gguluddene who was popularly known as Gguluddene meaning "Heaven is vast". Gguluddene lived for so long and he is believed to have lived for over 1000 years. He was followed by several kings who also lived for so long up to the reign of Bemba Musota, who was the last king of the Muwawa period. After the Muwawa period, Kato Kintu I's dynasty started and it has ruled Buganda up to the present day.

By the time of the Muwawa period, God had already taken away His presence from mankind. The leaders in the Muwawa period were only guided by angels of God who had godly powers. During this period, the traditional shrines had the right people who had godly powers. These were called High Priests "Bassenkulu" and Holy Priests "Bakabona". These helped people to interpret God's messages. After a very long period of time, the leaders in Buganda neglected this system and took the law in their hands including King Bemba-Musota the last leader of the Muwawa period.

King Bemba Musota became a tyrant, an oppressor and a dictator and this was not pleasing to God. He mistreated the people; he never followed the advice of his Council, disbanded the local Parliaments (Enkiiko) and executed some of the parliamentary members. He was rude with a hardy personality. His rule involved extra judicial killings, destruction of Holy Shrines, and absence of democracy, murder, torture and exiling of Princes. Because of this, God departed from him. Bemba Musota was a twin brother of Kato Kintu I. Actually his twin name was Wasswa hence Wasswa Bemba Musota and his twin brother was Kato Kintu I. It is Kato Kintu who overthrew his twin brother Wasswa Bemba-Musota with force of arms. This marked the beginning of the Kato Kintu I Dynasty.

When Wasswa Bemba Musota was King of Buganda, many people dis-associated with him because, he reared a big poisonous snake like an Anaconda which he used to station in front of his cave shelter. He used to sit behind in the rear of his cave, partitioned by a skin hide curtain and in front of it he stationed the humongous snake. Therefore people feared to go to his palace. People lived in agony and dire fright. They were mistreated and as such there was no peace in the Kingdom and its neighborhood.

Wasswa Bemba-Musota and his poisonous snake

His brother Kato Kintu I did not possess the spiritual will or zeal to fight his brother, who was a tyrant because he was not good in war skills. He had to go to Ethiopia and Egypt and get these skills and Godly powers. It was in these two countries that he was trained in warfare and effective administration. During this time, it was from those two countries Ethiopia and Egypt where Godly powers of anointment and war skills could be obtained. That is where Kato Kintu I went to get thorough training in leadership, military intelligence and fighting.

KABAKA KATO KINTU'S JOURNEY TO ETHIOPIA AND EGYPT

During that era and time, people used to travel on canoes along the river Nile Valley. In some places they used to travel on land. In Egypt and Ethiopia, he was taken into great palaces and Holy sacred shrines and he was accorded all respect as a Crown Prince. At the same time he was welcomed as a trading merchant, a teacher and a traveler and a tourist. His Majesty Kato Kintu I taught those people Buganda's culture and he also requested the Ethiopians and Egyptians to do the same. He was trained in war fare that is fighting using horses, the use of spy network, and use of explosives, bombs and leadership skills.

They took him into the holy shrines as the source of knowledge. They taught him the importance of councils such as; advisory councils, judicial councils, the council of elders, youth councils, the executive and legislative councils. He was also exposed to the Aliens. All these helped him and his men to acquire knowledge particularly leadership and warfare skills.

They also informed him that Buganda was a holy land and one of the origins of mankind. They also showed him migrants from Buganda to Egypt and Ethiopia namely the Abakeni, Abakanda and Abasongola. Amazing! These migrants' way of life was like that of the Baganda though there were some differences in colour.

His Majesty Kato Kintu I the King (Kabaka) took 4000 men with him who were trained in various skills. Kabaka Kintu was surprised on one occasion. As they were in one of those shrines in Egypt the spirit descended on one of the Auxiliary Bishops called Solomon and he spoke in Luganda the mother tongue of the Baganda!

The spirit directed them on military strategy and leadership skills. Kintu was educated that God's guidance and that of the Holy Spirit was the source of society transformation and enlightenment.

He was given confidence that although his brother Bemba Musota had a skilled army and well equipped force, they were going to assist him with the aerial knowhow, technology and fast moving vehicles.

King Kato Kintu I was exposed to many aspects of civilization like clothing and textiles, electricity, the Aliens and demi-gods. He was taught in skills of fighting using lightening and gunpowder. Kabaka Kintu spent 10 years in Ethiopia and Egypt and travelled back. He spent two years to and two years fro on this journey.

A map showing Kato Kintu I's journey from Buganda to Egypt.

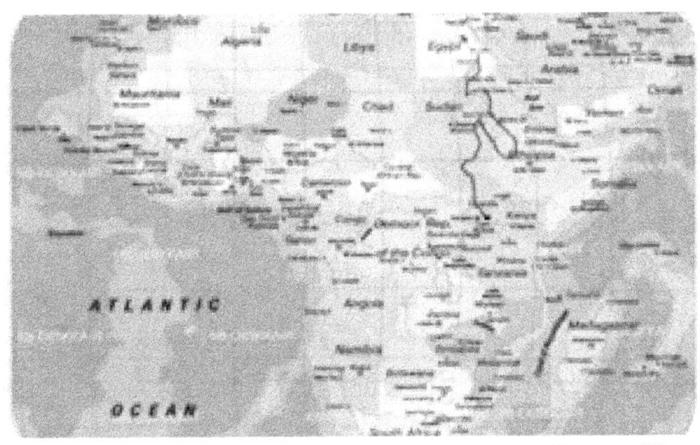

Courtesy Photo

THE BATTLE OF BLOOD BROTHERS KABAKA KATO KINTU I AND BEMBA MUSOTA TWIN BROTHERS AT WAR

On leaving Egypt and Ethiopia, His Majesty Kato Kintu I was given chariots and drivers, horses, hybrid seeds and so many other things. His Majesty Kato Kintu I embarked on his journey back to his country. By the standards of the time, His Majesty Kato Kintu I had graduated up to the level of a Field Marshal or a Doctor of Philosophy or PhD degree. He received a warm welcome in Buganda as a war hero much as he had changed in so many ways that is; dress code, appearance and conduct. His Majesty Kato Kintu I was peaceful, light skinned, tall, able bodied and above all a friendly Prince.

He was very much interested in the transformation of Buganda, believed in reconciliation and uniting people. He was an intelligent man, eager to learn new things, good at taking the advice of others, interested in research and new ideas, he was adventurous, ambitious, a great lover of sports, dance and music, he loved to respect culture, he was faithful and good at keeping covenants. In the course of the war, he promised people to bring fundamental changes in administration. He promised to restore an administration based on God's grace and people's will. His brother Bemba Musota had some divine powers and he was so skilled and believed to have been unconquerable. He had skilled soldiers, some were like demi-gods who used to disappear and reappear. They could forecast events to happen in future. On his return to Buganda His Majesty Kato Kintu I first camped in Ma-saaba in Mbale in Bugisu.

Photograph showing Kato Kintu I mobilizing warriors on mountain Elgon known as Masaaba in the local language

In Masaaba, he mobilized many people of various tribes and languages for example the Basoga, Banyoro, Bagishu, Japhadhola, the Bamba, the Banyole, the Basamya, the Bakedi, the Alur, the Bagweri and he created a very large army. It is from point that he travelled to Ddindo in Kyaggwe where he established a military camp. In Ddindo he united the other tribes including the Baganda in those areas, Abakooki, Abaziba, Abatoolo, Abakenyi, Abakedi, Bannakaragwe, Abakunta, Bannabuyaga, Abagangayizi and many others. He divided his army into units that is the spies, the infantry, cavalry, scribes, magicians, gunners and he then attacked his brother Bemba Musota.

Bemba Musota's military camp was at Kitala in Entebbe. In this place he had a special cave. When his men heard that Kato Kintu I had set off from Ddindo to attack, they began patrolling the land including the space. However, Kato Kintu I had changed his war strategy. He used guns and gun powder that he had got from Egypt and Ethiopia. He also used explosives which enabled him to threaten the enemy, Bemba Musota and his men. His enemies were not vast with this war technology.

Bemba Musota's men were on offensive all the time and they retreated up to Kabulamuliro. Kato Kintu I's infantry was too large spread up to Kasenge and another wing stretched up to Lake Victoria. It is believed that Kato Kintu I altogether had 1,000,000 soldiers armed with arrows, bows, spears, horses, explosives and spies.

All camps and settlements were set ablaze but, however, leaving escape routes for the enemy to retreat in which they engaged him. Most of Bemba Musota's men would fall into their traps and would be killed. There was serious fighting and many casualties were registered until when Bemba Musota was conquered and finally defeated. It was a total war in which brutal methods were used to kill people. It was terrible and the entire country was covered with blood and fear.

Map showing paces in which Kato Kintu I established military camps.

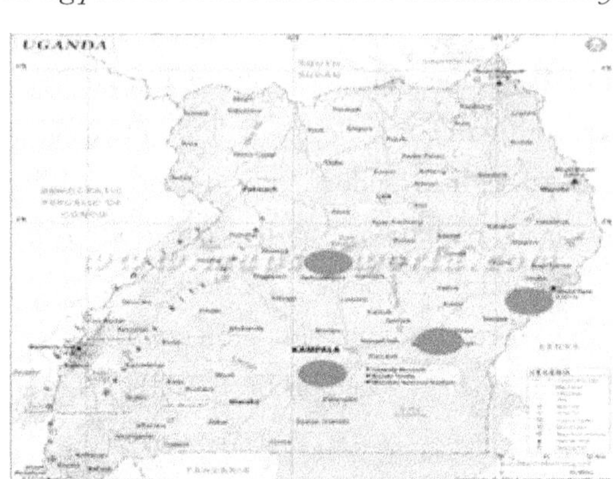

Courtesy Photo

In this battle some places were named after war events that took place. "Mawaanyi" in Bwebajja is remembered for fatal fighting where Bemba Musota had established road blocks. This place became known as Mawaanyi. Mawaanyi literary means a place surrounded with check-points. At "Kabulamuliro", many people died and settlements were destroyed, blazed and nothing that has life was spared. This place was named Kabulamuliro which means a cold place where no one is available to make fire again. The next town was named "Namulanda" which means the war spreads from one place to another. At this point even Bemba Musota's palace was destroyed and burnt to ashes. The next town was named "Kitala" which refers to the Arabian sword that was used by Kato Kintu I's army in defeating the enemy.

Serious fighting also took place in Kasenge - which means store or armory where weapons are stored. Kato Kintu I's scribes and magicians and wizards sent bees and ants to attack Bemba's soldiers. Such places were named Masanafu, Nakawuka and Kanjuki - all these are names of wild insects that bite and sting that were used in fighting Bemba Musota's army.

Bemba's soldiers were forced to retreat up to the King's palace at Kitala. Bemba Musota who was hiding in his cave with his snake was forced out because Kato Kintu I used explosives and gunpowder. Bemba was captured and his head was cut-off and his camp was completely destroyed. Bemba Musota's snake's head was also hacked off.

Kato Kintu I was crowned as King of Buganda. He established his head-quarters at Nnono in Busujju. He established a military fortification at Ntebbe Lunnyo. This place is where Mugula a psychic and a tribal lord used his super natural powers to curve seats out of rocks. At Nnono the legislative council sat and agreed on the values and norms that became Buganda's constitution and law although it was not written. The council was known as "Ttabamawanga" which literary means League of Nations. This marked the end of Bemba Musota's tyrannical rule and the Muwawa dynasty and the beginning of Kato Kintu I's dynasty.

LIST OF THE KINGS OF BUGANDA

1	Kato Kintu Early c.14th	Nnono, Busujju	Tamanyiddwa	Tamanyiddwa	Tekimanyiddwa
2	Ccwa I Mid c.14th	Unknown	Kintu	Nambi Nantuttululu	Ngeye
3	Kimera c.1374	Bumera, Busiro	Kalemeera*	Wannyana	Nseenene
4	Ttembo c.1404	Bujuuko, Busiro	Lumansi*	Nattembo	Mmamba
5	Kiggala c.1434	Ddambwe, Busiro	Ttembo	Najjemba	Ngonge
6	Kiyimba c.1464	Ssentema, Busiro	Kiggala	Nabukalu	Lugave
7	Kayima c.1494	Nnabulagala, Busiro	Wampamba*	Nakayima	Butiko
8	Nakibinge c.1524	Kkongojje, Busiro	Kayima	Nababinge	Mmamba
9	Mulondo c.1555	Bulondo, Busiro	Nakibinge	Namulondo	Butiko
10	Jjemba c.1564	Bubango, Busiro	Nakibinge	Najjemba	Ngonge
11	Ssuuna I c.1584	Gimbo, Busiro	Nakibinge	Nassuuna	Mmamba
12	Ssekamaanya c.1614	Kkongojje, Busiro	Mulondo	Nakku	Ffumbe
13	Kimbugwe c.1634	Bugwanya, Busiro	Ssuuna I	Nalugwa	Ndiga
14	Kateregga c.1644	Buteregga, Busiro	Ssekamaanya	Nabagereka	Butiko
15	Mutebi I c.1674	Kkongojje, Busiro	Kateregga	Namutebi	Mmamba
16	Jjuuko c.1680	Bujuuko, Busiro	Kateregga	Namutebi	Mmamba
17	Kayemba c.1690	Nabulagala, Busiro	Kateregga	Namutebi	Mmamba
18	Tebandeke c.1704	Bundeke, Busiro	Mutebi I	Nabukalu	Lugave
19	Ndawula c.1724	Musaba, Busiro	Jjuuko	Nandawula	Nseenene
20	Kagulu c.1734	Bbuga, Busiro	Ndawula	Nagujja	Njovu
21	Kikulwe c.1736	Kaliiti, Busiro	Ndawula	Nabikulwe	Ngo
22	Mawanda c.1738	Sserinnya, Busiro	Ndawula	Nakidde Luyiga	Ngo
23	Mwanga I c.1740	Kavumba, Busiro	Ggolooba Musanje*	Nabulya Nalugwa	Ndiga
24	Namugala I c.1741	Muyomba, Busiro	Ggolooba Musanje	Nabulya Nalugwa	Ndiga
25	Kyabaggu c.1750	Kyebando, Busiro	Ggolooba Musanje	Nabulya Nalugwa	Ndiga
26	Jjunju 1780	Luwunga, Busiro	Kyabaggu	Nanteza	Njovu

27	Ssemakookiro 1797	Kisimbiri, Busiro	Kyabaggu	Nanteza	Njovu
28	Kamaanya 1814	Kasengejje, Busiro	Ssemakokiro	Nansikombi	Nseenene
29	Ssuuna II 1832	Wamala, Kyaddondo	Kamaanya	Nakkazi Kannyange	Mmamba
30	Muteesa I 1856	Nabulagala, Kyaddondo	Ssuuna II	Muganzirwazza	Njovu
31	Mwanga II 1884	Nabulagala, Kyaddondo	Muteesa I	Baagalaayaze	Ngonge
32	Kiweewa 1888	Masanafu, Kyaddondo	Muteesa I	Kiribakka	Mmamba
33	Kalema 1888	Mmende, Busiro	Muteesa I	Ndibuwakanyi	Mmamba
34	Ccwa II 1897	Nabulagala, Kyaddondo	Mwanga II	Evelyn Kulabako	Ngabi
35	Muteesa II 1839-1969	Nabulagala, Kyaddondo	Ccwa II	Irene Namaganda	Nte
36	Mutebi II 1993	***	Muteesa II	Sarah Kisosonkole	Nkima

2
THE RACIAL MIX OF THE WORLD

From left to the right hand; Aliens, the Blacks, the Whites and the Chwezi

THE RACES

The White man is not a new creature on the African continent. Any assertion along these lines brings about assumption that Africa was discovered and brought out of the dark ages, yet these periods are timeframes. In the beginning of the entire creation, some spirits and angels were made to resemble the human shapes while others took other forms. Mankind was initially in soul form but was later dressed with the physical body then further varied in composition to form kinds. Out of the separation by God and His divine angels emerged four major classifications of the human race as below;

• The Blacks
• The Bachwezi (Yellow people)
• The Whites and the Reds
• The Aliens (Abamenke) i.e. The Greens

What people don't know is that God and Satan used to communicate and in direct communication to date though Satan disobeyed God. Like any other Institutions or Ministries within the Kingdom of God, Satan and his Ministry observe, give feedback and propose. At times the proposals are adopted as the Lord sees fit. So Satan suggested to God that mankind was a very wise creature more than anticipated and hence would be difficult to manage if left in a single grouping. This was the beginning of racial mix and separateness. The science of God's creation is concealed and mankind finds it puzzling. Satan operates as one of God's silent monitors for mankind and all other living creatures. The main duty is to give us protection. However, when you sin and disobey, Satan disorganizes your plans or may even kill you. This explains why the Baganda named Satan, Walumbe which literary means shadow of death. To God, the duty of Satan is to put mankind to test and to expose the inner side of souls. After putting you to test and you fall in his trap, he reports you to God, hence destroying your purity and relationship with God and hence Satan is paid for that duty. That is why people frequently say that it was the devil's work or I have fallen into Satan's temptation or it wasn't me! Man began to disobey God after 250 years of creation. After disobedience we were sent away from God's presence and from heaven because we ashamed God's image. Before disobedience we were in God's presence and God directly communicated with us. We were also united as one before the mix and the separateness. However the on goings of the world have brought further disintegration and mixing up more, generation after generation.

The best example that demonstrates this is that of the hybrid animals, cows and goats. Those brought from Europe or elsewhere by a donor to help disadvantaged communities. As time goes the hybrids crossbreed with indigenous species. With lapse of time the crossbreeds become real indigenous breeds. After a period let's say ten years, two indigenous breeds give birth to a real hybrid look alike. And then what looks like a real hybrid gives birth to a real local breed look alike.

Now, the question is, "Is the offspring a hybrid or a local breed?" That is where all the arguments and debates to-date emerge, in the world bringing about the confusion all over. The questions are, "How do two local breeds give birth to a hybrid? Then, how does that hybrid give birth to a hybrid? Then a buyer goes and buys two hybrids and after a period of time, those hybrids give birth to a local breed. The question again arises, how do two hybrids give birth to a local breed?" The answer is the hybrid was produced by a local breed. And also the buyer bought a local breed that was borne to a hybrid. That is the way it has been with people and hence the changes in the racial mixes.

This is not our plan but God's plan. Because different nations that emerge because of wanting to be independent, to the extent of forming new ways life and adopting new languages this does remove the racial separateness from the beginning, even despite the mixing being a continuous process. In some generations we may be the same and in others we are separated due to the inconstant situations such as wars, famine, diseases, search for greener pastures and other situations. It is common to find a black resembling a Chinese or Japanese or an Indian. On another occasion you may find a White resembling the blacks or an Ethiopian. Despite the different colors and racial mixes, all the people are the same in kind. What brings about the variations, are the different environments in which we live. It is therefore absurd to see that people and groupings fighting each other yet it is the same specie evolving despite the separateness and the racial mixes!

THE BLACKS

There are blacks in colour and blacks in heart. The blacks descend from Kintu and Nambi but not from Adam and Eve as it is alleged. Kintu and Nambi are blacks whose origin is Africa, for the most part Buganda. If you are tracing the origin of the blacks you move south and as you trace further, you will discover that the origin of all the blacks who are indigenous is Buganda. True blacks are known by the following features. They are beefy, short, able bodied and with a big nose. The blacks are hospitable, calm though sometimes short tempered. These include Baganda, Basoga, Banyoro, the Zulu, the Chagga, Rwenzululu, and Baziba, some Zimbabweans, some Nigerians and others.

THE WHITES AND REDS

The Reds may include the Japanese, Chinese, Koreans and others living in the seas or Oceania and on islands and also Indians much as they have variations due to environment.

The Whites may include the English, Italians, Russians or Germans de-pending on where they live. Many live in Europe but there are many, who appear different due to mix in bloodlines. There are those who are light skinned and those who are dark skinned. This comes as a result of intermarriages that are so common in the world.

THE YELLOWS-ABACHWEZI

These are common in the Arab World and the majority, are nomads if you want to quickly identify them. They have, however, spread to the entire world and they have intermarried with other races like in Congo, Somalia, Ethiopia, Malagasy, Suez Canal, Egypt, Buziba, Rwanda, Burundi, Nigeria but the majority is in Somalia and Ethiopia where they originate.

THE ALIENS OR THE GREENS

These are some of the salient features that describe the Aliens; pointed head structure, curved legs, big ears, somehow tall, very fast in action, they stammer, they are visionary, brevity, convincing, white hair , pale eyes, others have blue eyes and others have brown eyes. They are in most cases humble and they are devotees. They are in most cases dreamers, they are whiskers, they are principled and they respect people. They are hardworking, but they have greatly changed. They in most cases worship through the Divine powers of the White Angel of Life (Mukasa); the Red Angel of Power (Kiwanuka) and the Yellow Angel of Sense (Musoke). With the three, they are inseparable as value health, energy and knowledge. These people are found in countries like Wales, Britain, Germany, and Japhadhola areas in Eastern Africa, in Tibet, Bermuda areas and elsewhere.

The world has a mixture of races but the Aliens have their origin in Egypt, Ethiopia and America. They are of different types that we know and those that we do not know. These are facts though some people out of ignorance they distort the whole story. This race is not properly understood but the truth is that it exists together with other races as described in this book. However, alongside these Aliens we have described, there are those who are believed to be living in space on other planets. The Aliens who live on earth resemble other races somehow in appearance. There are some Aliens that home in water bodies such as, America in California, New Jersey and Bermuda where they have sanctuaries underneath, where they come up with many discoveries of technology.

Photo showing how the Aliens from other planets look like

Courtesy Photo

THE TRAVELLORS / THE SETTLERS / THE IMPERIALISTS

These are described in Kiswahili language as the Mzungu which literary means traveler or loiterer. Because these Whites especially from Europe and America were mobile; the indigenous Africans named them Bazungu meaning somebody who loiters from one place to another. These were mainly from the Arab World and Europe. What was amazing is that natives found it difficult to differentiate and identify them although the visitors were able to identify each other. They generally speak through the nose. Because they spoke from the nose the Baganda used to refer to them as Abaluŋŋaana because their voice intonation was similar to the sound of a hornbill. These came to Africa to exploit the commercial advantages that Africa could offer to their countries. Because Africa looked 20 like a treasury house full of material wealth, they came and took colonial possessions on behalf of their home countries.

The first Whiteman believed to come to Buganda was John Hannington Speke in 1862. This was during the administration of King Muteesa I. He wanted to see the source of River Nile and use it a stepping stone to take all the states in the Nile Valley especially Egypt which was a land of great civilization and always an eminent danger to their co-existence. In the process, he landed on Buganda which was also a great and mighty Kingdom south of the Sahara.

Photo of John Hannington Speke

IN MEMORY OF
SPEKE
VICTORIA NYANZA
AND THE NILE
1864

Courtesy Photo

John Hannington Speke arrived at Nyanza and saw a huge lake with fresh water and he named it Lake Victoria. It is known by that name up to the present day. People falsely say that he is the one who discovered that lake yet the truth is that he was not the first White man or visitor to see it. The truth is that this lake existed even before him and the Baganda knew this lake and it was known as Lake Nalubaale which literary means the 21 sanctuary of holy souls.

Surprisingly, 700 years from his time in 1160AD, there is an Arab Muslim missionary and a geographer, an astrologist and a cartographer who came to the region and explored this lake and drew its map. By the time Speke and other explorers came to Buganda, they knew this fact and that is why the put so much emphasis on the Mountains of the Moon, because if you reached the Mountains of the Moon (Mt. Ruwenzori) then it would be easier to find the source of the Nile and hence able to control Egypt, that was an agitating thorn in their boots.

This Arab explorer was known as Muhammad Ibin Idrisi and was believed to have been a very wise intelligent man. His maps he made are not so different from those made by John Hannington Speke and other explorers who came after 700 years. Imagine!

Photo of Muhammad Ibin Idrisi

Courtesy Photo

During the administration of Ssekabaka Kamaanya in the early 1800s, there also is a White man called Koffi who came to Buganda. Koffi used to travel on an elephant. He travelled around the Continent doing drawings and paintings while distributing coffee seedlings to the people. These travelers were volunteers who ventured into other parts of the world on their own without government support. Such people were greatly respected and venturing and exploration became a symbol of prestige and greatness to people who did such voluntary work on behalf of their home governments.

"Adam" means capacity to co-create, to cause continuity while "Eve" means mother of nations. Adam and Eve had two children Cain and Abel. God asked them to offer burnt offerings to him as sacrifice. Abel offered sheep and Cain offered produce of land. Cain's offering was well received by God but God accepted Abel's offering and sacrifice. Cain killed his brother instead of putting right his mistake. This to God was a mark of great disobedience. Cain's race was cursed by God and a permanent mark was left on the descendants for easy identification!

In the bible it is said that Cain left the Garden of Eden after killing his brother Abel. He travelled in the North and went to East of Eden in the land of the Nod. Cain produced children among the Nod and he also built a city which he named Enoch after his first born. This means that other races existed, otherwise how did Cain produce children? He couldn't have married his sisters! Who lived in the city that he built? What about the people he found in this country? What was their origin? These could have either been the descendants of Kintu and Nambi who are the blacks or other racial mixes such as the Yellow race, Red or the Alien races etc. It is probable that it was one of these races since he had killed his only brother, meaning that the Blacks or other groups existed which do not come from Adam and Eve, who are the birth parents of the White race. Secondly these groups have never been alien to each other but have rather been known to each other from beginning and have always mixed and intermarried from time to time, to date. It is therefore a falsehood to suggest that we all come from Adam and Even yet there a distinct racial separateness.

3
ANCIENT KINGDOMS

Earthly kingdoms are institutions or vehicles in which the message of God descends or God's will is manifested to the people with legitimate leadership, divine spiritual agents, spiritual covenants and God's Sanctuary within it. For example Saudi Arabia is a kingdom but this kingdom has God's Sanctuary which is Mecca.

Kingdoms are formed and transformed depending on God's plan and power and how God's manifests himself in that particular region to make that place the sanctuary of his power. This is similar to the uneven distribution of wealth in different countries of the world. Some countries are much endowed with resources while others are not. Some countries are blessed with good climate while others are not. Therefore, even God's power is manifested differently in different kingdoms or places according to his plan as we shall discuss later.

The Principal Spirit thus Mwene meaning Chief or Overseer is the Prime Coordinator within the Institution of the Holy Spirit (Mwoyo Kitiibwa). Therefore, from the Holy Spirit, below is Mwene the Principal Spirit who performs prime ministerial duties within the Ministry and Institution of the Holy Spirit. Since the Principal Spirit is Head in formulation of Ministries and departments to perform various duties in instituting the Kingdom of God and will on Earth and elsewhere; the Leadership framework is instituted through Trinity of the following vehicles; God's will in the people and way of life – Mukasa (Peoples); God's will through the Heads – Ndawula (Chiefs) and lastly but not least, God's will through his messengers or Holy Priests – Sseggululigamba, which when all are combined account for the variations in nature of the existing earthly kingdoms on how God's will is manifested in those places. It also accounts for the level and type of anointment in terms of strength and enlightenment of the various communities or groups. Below, the earthly kingdoms operate within the framework of the given Trinity for that particular place and hence to those people it is a covenant of God within God's sanctuary in that kingdom or place. Other messengers of God operate following the values, norms and traditions of the people because these are the heritages to be followed.

DESCRIPTION OF THE TRINITY WITH IN THE KINGDOM MUKASA

The institution of Mukasa within the kingdom directs conduct among those people or persons to enable well-being; moral being and a spiritual way of life of the setup with the parameters that are required by God. The Baganda since time immemorial had songs of praise for the institution as shown below;

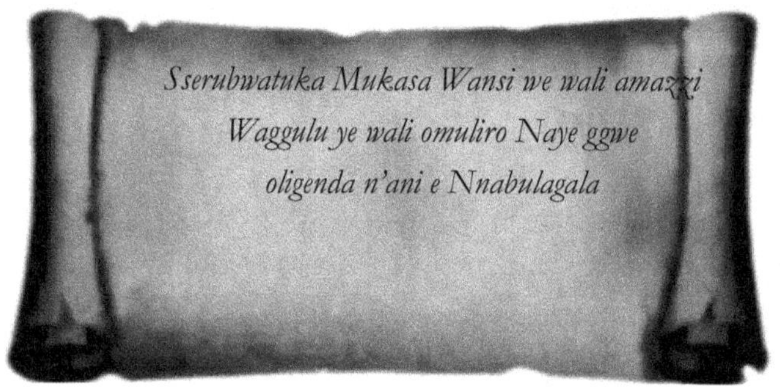

The interpretation of the song is;

Mukasa the great one, most powerful,
You are engulfed with water below,
You are guarded with fire above.
Who will ever cause death to you as you are stronger
than the doors of hell?

The people in Buganda know Mukasa as an institution. He is the spirit of stored life that blesses them with children and when someone is blessed with a child, they will always say "Bweza bwa Mukasa", meaning let the name of the Mukasa Institution be glorified. Mukasa is also known as the Institution that produces rain and gives bumper harvests. It is believed world over that water is life, which means even Mukasa as an Institution is in charge of water and rain. He is the giver of productive life by the power of God Almighty. Mukasa causes the messengers of God to have dreams and in the dreams they get the message of God for the people.

Kabaka Mukasa, the angel guides people in their clans because spiritually they are his children and he passes on God's message and orders people to set up shrines (Amasabo) for the worshiping of God and glorification of His Name. The shrines are managed by the High Priests (Bassenkulu). Mukasa's spirit sits on the Priests to act as medians and gives them orders to execute God's will. The Priests give the messages to the in charge (clan head or Omu-taka w'ekiggwa) who in turn give the messages to the presiding King.

Kabaka is the King in the human body and he is given the name Kabaka which means receiver of the message for the people. Mukasa is the Spiritual King for Buganda; who in his spiritual form is the link between God and the Kabaka and the people. The message he brings to the people is intended to create order within the Clans and the Kingdom. Every Clan Head has a shrine for his clan (Ekiggwa ky'ekika) managed by a High Priest (Ssenkulu) and a Holy Priest (Kabona). These work hand in hand. The Clan Heads gather the information they have got from their shrines and they give it to the King. The King publically announces such information to the people.

The institution of Mukasa is life because he gives and sustains breath. He is the breath of life in air, water, in space, underground and in all living organ-isms, be it plants and animals. Mukasa's breath has types; the dew that enables plants other living things to grow and multiply, the rain that supplies water to the lakes, rivers, rain clouds, in the space and on land and the unknown. The angel that Heads the Institution is also known as Mukasa or Spirit Angel. The rain and water supplied by Mukasa generally helps living organisms to live everywhere on land, in space, in lakes, rivers, ponds and underground. He controls the winds, the storms, the dew and the rain. When mankind disobeys God, and since Mukasa is a sustainer of life, Mukasa uses the winds and the storm to destroy all living creatures and the earthly kingdom (Obwakabaka) especially when people do not want to take the advice of God's messengers. The survivors then will have a story to tell to the other generations about the dangers of disobeying God. However mankind is not a trouble-free creature. You may find that after a while, mankind will go back into disobedience. When God sees this He punishes mankind as He did to his forefathers, because God is the same yesterday, today and tomorrow. Mankind and other living creatures are not immortal, they can be destroyed, they can wither and perish but the will of God is immortal and lives forever.

NDAWULA

The Ndawula institutions are the branches or the different institutions or departments in which the leadership or stewardship powers of God are manifested to mankind. God's sanctuary within the kingdoms has other many departments and sub-departments which help to transplant God's power of stewardship from one place to another in the entire kingdom.

People in Buganda say that the Ndawula institution spreads like a hydra and why the Baganda love their King (Kabaka) and their Kingdom so much is because they know that they are directly connected to God through such institutions. The great love the people have for the Kabaka their King, the great respect that is accorded to him are because people in Buganda know that their King is a shadow of God. He represents God. When the King disobeys God's Trinity as described in this book, his kingdom becomes disorganized, many problems come, many wars come, his people may turn against him and he may also be deposed or overthrown through force of arms. The Kingdom may experience many natural calamities like floods, strange diseases, moral degeneration, bloodshed, drought and famine.

The Ndawula institution is created by God and there are many creatures embedded within it both living and nonliving things, the tangible and the abstract. Apart from the storm that is abstract, you may find many things including mountains, hills and rocks, calabashes, hens, goats, some rep-tiles, forests all dedicated to belong to the Ndawula Institution.

This spirit gets an individual from within the kingdom and consecrates him or her and gives the person authority to execute its duties intended to fulfill the will of God. The consecrated person becomes the Commander or Spiritual Counsel who is made to reside in reach of the King's palace as a representative of the Institution of Ndawula. This Spiritual Counsel is also called Ndawula. The most well-known of such people are Ndawu-la Ggoogombe, Ndawula Lukanga and Ndawula Kyalublmba. As a matter of course such a person that represents Ndawula's spirit (Chief of Kings Angel) which is referred to as Kabaka Ndawula meaning Chief of Kings' Angel. The representative is called Katebe meaning the one that officiates, Ndawula's throne. He is also at times referred to as Kabaka Ndawula meaning Chief in the Institution of Ndawula. Because he has his official position and mantle, and out of custom it is not permissible for him to sit or preside on the King's throne or official seat called Namulondo. It is also a taboo for Kabaka Ndawula to go to the palace of the ruling King, because he is also a Chief representing the Ndawula Institution and its Angel.

The Ndawula Institution and its divine spirit is part of God's trinity whose major duty is to give the King or presiding leader advice and to guide him on how to manage Kingdom affairs. Katebe is regarded as a Prince who is also the head of all the priests within the institution, and performs all rituals on behalf of the King. That is why the Baganda say the King does not perform any ritual because he has Katebe who does the needful while following guidance accorded by the Chief of Kings institution.

When the institution of Ndawula is despised, many aspects of leadership in the kingdom become disorganized and the kingship (Namulondo) may be removed completely. Many institutions of kingship, and traditional leaderships, have separated themselves from God's covenant in the world have been destroyed or disorganized. There are many in Asia, Europe and there are many in Africa like Ethiopia, Egypt, Zulu, Busoga, Ankole, Zanzibar and Kiziba. What could be the reason for their destruction? It is because of the disassociation caused by departure from the original or traditional setup with-in these Kingdoms. You may find that there are some small kingdoms that have exist within big states. What makes the mighty kingdoms to be destroyed like that of Haile Salase, King Herod that were known and no effort has been made to have them revived? What could be the cause?

The bad thing is also when the Katebe who represents the Ndawula Angel poses as a King or turns against the King, yet his duty is to bring the message from the Chief of Kings Institution to the King. When this happens, the Angel takes it upon herself to obliterate the Representative and consecrates another Katebe. He may become crippled; he may develop mental illness and other disorders and become obsolete. The Angel or Spirit brings many diseases, many problems and calamities and moral decay.

SSEGGULULIGAMBA

The Sseggululigamba Institution is referred to as Voice of Heaven. The Baganda call the Angel, Kabaka Sseggululigamba. The Angel heads all spirits that do work within the Institution in performing messianic duties on behalf of God. The Baganda are knowledgeable of the fact that all Prophets (Abalubaale or Balubaale) fall under of the jurisdiction of this Ministry. The message conveyance of the Voice of Heaven Institution is done with support of another Institution; which is the Sense Ministry headed by the Rainbow / Sense Angel (Musoke) to beef up and stream-line the message so that it goes out to the recipients with articulacy. The Sense Institution like any other Ministries falls under direct authority of the Holy Spirit that comes from the one true God. The departmentalization of various Institutions and assignment of tasks is under mandate of the Overseer Angel (Mwene) who performs prime ministerial functions under the Institution of the Holy Spirit.

The Voice of Heaven Institution (Sseggululigamba) sends other Angels or Spiritual Agents such as those from Attorney General's Institution called Nnende whose role is to interpret and weigh the nature of the messages to be delivered and also determine what is necessary for that that place where work is to be done. The Spiritual Agents from Attorney General's.
Institution of God convey their messages to and through other Ground spirits or Planet Caretaker Spirits known as Chief Elders (Mmandwa) and the messengers of God known as Prophets to put right all wrongs in society. Every Prophet is given a guardian angel to keep him in path of God and help him not to distort the message. The messengers, who divert from the path of God and backslide, sometimes fall from grace. God has been sending his messages through such prophets, generation after generation in different regions.

The spirits or angels such as described above bestow different gifts upon prophets or those carrying out duties in conveying God's messages. Some people are given power to get messages through dreams, others through prophecy, through getting visions, others interpret signs and events; and others are able to foretell all by the power of the same spirit. Others through the same spirit are adorned with power to perform miracles or be beyond belief such as flying in space, walking on water, appearing and disappearing instantly etc.

When the Kabaka or King of Buganda gets the messages from various sources as some of the above, he tries to implement the remedy in his Kingdom. If he refuses to put into practice the warnings, then this be-comes his fault if he gets troubles.

The Voice of Heath Institution (Sseggululigamba) links all those Priests who have the gift of prophecy to the Sense Institution called Musoke. The Musoke Institution is also called the Rainbow Ministry. The Rainbow Ministry or Sense Institution fills them with wisdom and understanding that comes from God. Then they give these messages to the people. In Buganda these Prophets are called Balubaale or Abalubaale. Every Prophet comes with the message given to him directly to the people to put right what is wrong that was not put right by the first generations or forefathers. These Prophets are sometimes despised, which then becomes the root cause of trouble for those nations.

The prophets (Balubaale) act as the voice of God and they speak his word as they are guided by his spirit. The Holy Spirit is the integral part of all departments that perform God's work. Therefore, despising the Prophets of God or annihilating them by whatever methods, the Power of the Trinity i.e. the Spirit Institution of Mukasa; The Chief of Kings Ministry of Ndawula and The Voice of Heaven Ministry of Sseggululigamba will automatically destroy and erase any perpetrator(s) because their power is beyond human understanding. Their power of destruction can only be compared to that of an earth shattering Tsunami!

Satan has played an important role in shaming mankind, by influencing mankind to act inhumanly and hence making mankind social misfits. People focus on miracles performed by their fellow human beings instead of focusing on God's holiness. Believing in God is all about being faithful, focusing on his goodness, holiness, love for one another, unity, hard work and patience but not miracles. This is because miracles can be performed by people who do not act on behalf of God.

The moment you realize that some people who claim to serve God are proud, greedy, hate each other, liars, killers, exploiting others, sabotaging others and not sticking to the agreements they make with others, although they pull crowds just know that what they are doing is ungodly and following them will lead you to destruction. Taking poison because it is sweet does not make it honey. The moment you realize it is poison, abandon otherwise your life ceases to exist. No one can be blamed for your deeds. Do not focus only on the fruits, but also the roots.

SUMMARY ON EARTHLY KINGDOM (BUGANDA)

The trinity we have talked about; the Spirit Institution (Mukasa), the Chief of Kings Institution (Ndawula) and the Voice of Heaven Institution (Ssegululigamba) send their spiritual messenger to help the reigning Kabaka who fulfills all rituals for the Kingdom called Kabaka Lukenge. Lukenge spirit or angel helps the King to foresee the events to come in future and present. Sometimes he is called Mutebi because the two names literary mean to foretell or to foresee. The King of Buganda is known by the name, Maasomoogi to mean somebody who is sharp and critical of every detail and therefore able to anticipate events. The symbol for both the Voice of Heaven Ministry and Chief of Kings Ministry is that of a lion. This is why the King of Buganda is referred to as a lion.

Lukenge is an angel from heaven to perform the duty of an adviser to the King or the Kabaka. The moment the Kabaka is crowned, it symbolizes that all the Clan Heads have conferred all spiritual blessings and powers onto the Crowned King. During coronation the crown prince is made to perform rituals such as; the nighttime drills referred to as the, "Nighttime war against evil (Olutalo lw'ebirumbirumbi)" which rituals are meant to get the new reign free of evil. If the King fails to perform the drills to satisfaction, then he is not crowned.

Every Clan Head has a duty to perform his set of rituals on the Crown Prince. In Buganda Kingdom, every person belongs to a clan including the King himself. Every clan has a designated Holy Shrine and every Clan Head is Head of Worship in their respective clans and are therefore adorned with special powers in their regard, and that is why at the time of Coronation they are very essential in conducting the coronation, as spiritual representatives for their clans. Since the Clan Heads or Lords (Abataka) have conferred powers onto the Crown Prince, the Crown Prince then becomes Head of all the Clans hence Ssabataka. The King is sworn in, traditional prayers are conducted and many rituals are performed, and then the King is made to receive the covenant. When he is sworn in, he makes a spiritual agreement with God to fulfill God's covenant, to be faithful and to bear true allegiance to the people, to give fair judgment and protect his people and country and all the things emphasized by Clan Heads during the coronation ceremony.

After coronation, the Kabaka i.e. King performs many rituals which are secret in nature and therefore cannot be voiced. After coronation he is taken to a traditional house called Bwanika which means "to expose", to swear that he will never deviate from the covenant outlined in this book.

From this house it is all jubilation with sounds of the royal drums called Mujaguzo. The King amidst such celebrations and jubilation is made to beat the royal drum called Mutimagwansi (Heart of the Nation) or Buganda or Ntunnunsi as he swears not to deviate from the covenant, that he will always fight like a brave man for his country; he swears to work hand in hand with his people; and he swears to keep good diplomatic relationship with his neighbors.

After this ceremony, the members of the Buffalo Clan carry him up on their shoulders to the official seat Namulondo. He is encircled by the people. The priests give him a spear; they dress him in the leopard skin and that of a lion. At the throne (Namulondo) he is made to sit on lion skin and below the throne the place is decorated with skin hides of other animals. Then he is dressed in robes and in his waist he is strapped tightly and laced with a knot in the neck to symbolize being brave and not to be afraid of adversaries or challenges.

Then the Clan Heads, the Priests and others with spiritual powers per-form the ritual of coronation. All the Baganda present form a ring fence round the Crown Prince and hold each other's hands from those in the inner ring outwards to the last circle. These are the last stages of coronation and anoint-ment where the joining of hands for all those present, to the Priest who is crowning, all are conferring blessings collectively upon the Prince who is to sit as the reigning King. This symbolism and acts at the time of crowing is a final mark to the Lord that the Nation has entered a covenant with the new leader who is to be their King. They lift the crown and put it on his head to symbolize that the entire country or Kingdom has agreed and crowned him according tradition. He is then shown to the people and it is declared that he is now the new King and he is given many titles such as Maasomoogi, Beene, Nnatawetwa, Ssaabataka and many others.

There are three strange signs, miracles or things that must happen on the day to mark the success of the coronation ceremony. There is always a strike of lightning and thunder, it rains and signs of the rainbow cover the entire sky. This symbolizes that the trinity of Holy Spirit; Mukasa or Spirit life, Musoke or Sense Spirit and Kiwanuka or Power Spirit; have passed the bestowing of the spirit of Lukenge upon the Reigning King. The Kabaka is anointed with special powers that are electrifying and even when speaks his voice sounds special and seems to hit a cord with listeners as if he is addressing their inner souls. When he talks you automatically know that it is the King speaking and when you get closer to him you feel something very unusual. After this, what-ever the King says you see it as a blessing. This is why whenever the King gives an order people reply Wampa Ssebo or Gusinze Ssaabasajja implying that, "let it be as you say" or "at your pleasure my Majesty". This is because the Kabakaship or kingship does not belong to human beings but it belongs to God. The people belong to the Kabaka and when they work closely with him it makes him and the institution very safe.

WHY ARE KINGDOMS DISORGANISED AFTER SPRITUAL LIBERATION

God made arrangements for leadership for different regions, states and king-doms depending on the nature of the region, depending on the needs of the people and he gave them appropriate leadership to make them live in peace. God created people differently so they have different aspirations, cultures, beliefs and life standards, values, norms and cultures. Therefore this means different people have different ways of communicating with their God. This is what they call peace and hence they call this God's fairness.

When you disintegrate this arrangement which people perceive as God's fair-ness and you bring another system that they don't know and you re-move the type of leadership people are used to, the society you intended to liberate, becomes disorganized. This is exactly what the self-imposing masters did in our societies. Therefore, it is for that reason that people have to follow the grand plan of God for them. Every nation has its destiny according to God's arrangement and thus unique in its ways ranging from the basic of requirements like food up to things like leadership styles which all collectively become their culture and tradition.

CATEGORIES OF LEADERSHIP IN THE EARTHLY KINGDOMS

GOD'S MANIFESTATION	CHARACTERISTICS
1. Republican	• Elections by Vote • Leader swears an oath
2. Two Tier System	• Spiritual Leader • Political Leader
3. Clan System	• Leadership through Groupings • Worship in groupings
4. The Sanctuaries	• Direct Rule by God

REPUBLICAN SYSTEM

This is referred to as the Zero system and people's power in the systems is in the fact that everybody is equal to the other like the Zero number. Such people use one of these systems like the unitary type of government or the republican system. They choose leaders from within themselves depending on his skills and ability. They choose a leader with qualities that God desires, he or she swears an oath and they make him or her leader. By majority vote such a person becomes the leader who rules the country in peace and unity.

LEADERSHIP STYLE COUPLED WITH THE CHIEF OF KINGS MINISTRY

The power of God works hand in hand with monarchy or existing leader-ship system. The difference is that God and the spiritual Kingdom has a representative specifically from the Ndawula Ministry of God that deals with leadership matters such providing counsel within the Kingdom of God and elsewhere as seen fit and that is why it is referred to as the Chief of Kings Ministry. So, alongside the sitting Monarch is a High Priest from Ministry who gives counsel to the ruler on behalf of God, the Ministry and the people so that people are governed within those parameters required by God. This means that God rules the Kingdom together with the King (Kabaka) in streamlining the state. The leadership of the King or Kabaka is legitimate and the King comes from the royal family. When you set up artificial chiefs and priests who are not legitimate, automatically you disorganize that society. This is the link between God, the spiritual world, the kingdom or state leadership and the people. The spiritual seat is given special status within the Kingdom or State. The best example is the lineage of King Solomon and King David in Judea.

THE CLAN SYSTEM (BWAMUKASA)

The power of God works hand in hand with the clans and such societies or kingdoms are ruled by clan heads or elders. Clan heads are the leaders of society and the overall leader is the Ssabataka (Kabaka or head of clan heads). The leadership in this system works on clans and their heads. Every clan is a grouping of worship and how they use it to reach out to God to get counsel, direction and protection. Every clan has headquarters, and an official shrine for worship. The clan leader is the head of spiritual affairs within the clan and he is known as Omutaka as a title and Omukulu wa Kasolya when it comes to spiritual matters. The shrine has a High Priest (Ssenkulu) and a Holy Priest (Kabona). The people's connection to God is through the Holy Shrines, which Holy Places are also accessible to the ruler for counsel and direction. When you change this system you bring so many problems. The link between mankind and God begins in the royal shrines and the clan system setup because that is how they remedy their challenges; get fairness, protection and livelihood.

THE SANCTUARY (EKITEBE)

These are places or states that have areas with sanctuaries of God. These places have a distinct leadership, a distinct people with a unique moral foundation and generally set apart as a people. The leadership works hand in hand with God's messengers who fall in the three categories, earlier explained as the Trinity of manifestation of God's leadership powers into earthly kingdoms or states.

Ndawula's Representative. This is where the King or ruler or leadership has a representative directly from God's Institution of Leadership to give counsel on spiritual and leadership to enable society thrive fairly and in harmony, while fulfilling God's purpose and plan. The Counsel acts as a representative from God's Institution of Leadership; called Ndawula and here in Buganda is called he called Katebe meaning "Divine Seat" or Kabaka Ndawula.
The Mukasa Institution is where the clan heads head their clans and they create a link between man and God right from the Clan Temples where they receive spiritual direction and assistance.

The Sseggululigamba Institution, where the Holy Priests (Prophets) and other messengers of God are attached to the Holy Sanctuary or Spiritual Control Center of that place and also endowed with the gift or blessing of carrying God's word to the People or doing God's work, on behalf of God to the people.
This trinity works collaboratively to direct the leaders on God's grand plan to

lead society justly and effectively. In most cases where there is a Sanctuary or Seat of God within the area or state, the Trinity is manifested in its complete form while other areas may have one, two or the three facets depending on God's plan. Some of the known Sanctuaries can be found in Saudi Arabia, Japan, Buganda, Britain, Rome, Greece and some other places.

All in all, in a Republican area, the elected leader takes an oath using one of the Holy Books to govern his people fairly, effectively and in harmony and therefore enters a covenant with the people and God. If the leader veers off from the right path his leadership starts having unexplainable problems and considered cursed by the people. However, in the monarchial system the area could either have one of the three (i.e. the Katebe, the Clan Heads or Lords and Prophets or Messengers), or the two or all. The Sanctuary or Seat of God is bonus but exists where Kingdoms are or used to exist! This is why it is said in the Lord's Prayer, "Thy Kingdom come onto earth as it is in Heaven!" The Sanctuary is a storage center for sacred knowledge and sacred power.

4
THE COVENANTS

Mankind was so special before God and his Holy Spirit. The angels of God at the time got on well with mankind because there was less burden brought by mankind unlike the present day. God loved to care for man-kind like caring for a young child who has just learnt to speak, to walk, to talk and to play. The Holy Spirit and angels of God played a supportive role in enabling man to do various activities with ease, such as; being creative, treating ailments with quick recovery, speedy learning, doing the extraordinary like walking on water and flying in space, being able to manipulate animal transportation such as dragons, elephants etc., anticipating events promptly through dreams, forecasting and foretelling and so on and so forth.

Man lost this special relationship with God after his disobedience and God decided to punish him. However, at times God either turns a blind eye and lets things pass as he sees fit, or forgives when man repents and turns to right paths of God. In the process of repentance man makes new covenants with God never to sin again or repeat the same mistake which has become a norm among us and the other races.

The disobedience of man comes as a result of Satan's disagreement with God's plan of creation. Satan's duty is to give God information about our inequities showing God how we are sinners. However, sometimes people who are strong and committed to God resist Satan. The major aim of Satan is to put you to test to prove whether you have trust in God or not. When you fall into his traps or temptation he reports you to God. That is how Satan has been putting mankind into problems. However, all covenants made, whether in daily lives or spiritual in nature, in God's presence they are registered and stand as mutual agreements provided they yield good intent.

An agreement is mutual understanding. Covenants are of many types. There are spiritual covenants that mankind makes with God. There are spiritual covenants between clans and God. There are covenants between individuals but making God a witness. Making a covenant is putting a condition. Sometimes it is a promise, sometimes is to repent never to do something again. Covenant is like putting pen on paper by confirmation of a signature making a promise before God that if he does something for you, you will also do something or give something in return. If God answers your prayers and you do not fulfill the agreement you made with him, it means you have broken the covenant. You become a liar and this means you have a case to answer before God. This means you have broken God's command which says; "Thou shall not tell lies". All other laws line up against this one. When you act out of the covenant it means you take responsibility. The Baganda have made the following covenants with or before God;

THE COVENANT OF GOD AND KINTU KITAKA NAWANSI KYAWADDA I

The first covenant was from Kintu Kitaka Nawansi Kyawadda I with his wife Nambi Nantuttululu Aliweebwa Nabitaka. This covenant was made after the dual had sinned against God and he gave them principles on which to live. This was after Nambi and Kintu fulfilled sexual pleasures in the holy places and they hid themselves from God after falling into Satan's temptation. God needed man to consult him before doing anything. Man had to wait for God's order before any action.

Nambi had a child and named it Walulumba Sooka and the Angel of the shadow of death killed him, on the orders of God. This disobedience was not only among the blacks but also among other races. All of them were sent away from heaven and God hid his presence from mankind.

After realizing that he had sinned, Kintu remorsefully bowed down before

God together with his wife and said, "We are Sorry' Satan tempted us and convinced us that we didn't need your permission to procreate". God sent them away saying "Go and labour with this world".

After Kintu pleading so much before God, he was given Ten Orders and Commandments to observe. Since God was no longer reachable, a prophetic spirit would descend unto Kintu's son, Mazzi Ganda and give direction and guidance. This became the order where they would congregate, worship, repent, wait spiritual direction and proclaim the ten orders and the Ten Commandments as a mark of renewal.

There is nothing in this world that was without a stipulation; Mankind was given two hands with ten fingers, the ten fingers to represent God's ten orders and two feet with ten toes, the ten toes to remind mankind the ten commandments;

GOD'S ORDERS	
1. HEAVENAND EARTH	•SIGNIFICANCE OF GOD IN HEAVEN AND MANKIND ON EARTH
2. GOD'S POWER	• HIS WILL
3. GOD'S INSTITUTIONS	• GOD'S MINISTRIESAND THE HEADS IN THE KINGDOM OF GOD.
4. PIRITUAL POLICY GUARDIANS ORANGELS	• POLICYAND PLAN KEEPERS

5. KEEPERS OR AUXIALIARY SPIRITS	• GOD'S ARMY TO PROTECT GOD'S AGENDA
6. SOULS	• EVERY CREATION IS ASOUL
7. YOUR PLACE	• WHERE YOU LIVE,ADAPT
8. NATION	• YOUR BELONGING IS YOUR GROUPING
9. LEADERSHIP	• ORDER OF COMMAND
10. YOUR LINEAGE OR CLAN	• YOUR ROOTS

GOD'S COMMANDMENTS

1. ONE GAIN, ONE LOSS NEVER UNDERESTIMATE

2. PAST IS PAST, NOT REASON TODAY

3. REMOVE THE UNNECESSARY IN YOUR PLANS

4. IT NEEDS ANEW PLAN ACCORDINGLY

5. FIND NEW WAYS AND MAKE RESEARCH

6. DO NOT DISTURB AKEEPER BECAUSE HE IS
   A STARTING POINT

7. REMOVEALL BLOCKS

8. HOW CAN YOU BECOME CLEAN?

9.WHERE YOU RELATE, IS IT THE RIGHT PLACE?

10. NOW PUT FIRE INALLAFFAIRS FOR MEAND YOU.

Observing the orders of God is equivalent to the glorification of His name, His power and respect for His messengers, angels and spirits. The commandments of God require us to respect our leaders, our environment, appreciating the wonders of God's creation, living in unity, love and peace, respecting cultural norms and values in a civil way so that we can enjoy the fruits of world in harmony, that God has given us.

SSEKABAKA NAKIBINGE'S SPIRITUAL COVENANT

King Nakibinge of Buganda had his administration characterized by crisis and revolution. His administration was characterized by wars, dis-eases, famine and drought plus many calamities that you can talk about.

King Nakibinge of Buganda was a great leader with profound history. He was 49, a warrior and war hero. However his traditional enemies had become a problem because they had proved unconquerable. This was a period of state formation, expansion and consolidation.

One day he summoned a consultative meeting with his administrative council to inquire whether any of them had any strategy to save Buganda from its many enemies. His high ranking military general Kimbowa was also in attendance. One of his subjects that was sat, near Kimbowa the General stood up and advised to lead the delegation to Ssese islands to consult Omutaka Wannema who was the highest priest with spiritual and prophetic powers of God. He was informed that this priest, Wannema had his son whose name was Kyobe Kyomubazzi who was a great warrior and a fighter with spiritual powers, could help him fight his enemies.

The King followed this advice and together with his delegation reached Ssese Islands where, they were taken to Wannema's shrine.

During this time Wannema was the greatest Priest in the shrines of the Pulse or Earthquake Angel (Musisi), the White Angel (Mukasa) and Yellow angels (Musoke) who are of great significance within Buganda way of worship. Wannema refers to the baggage angel, and therefore Wannema was an Auxiliary Bishop for the Baggage Angel that represents the disabled institution within the Kingdom of God. He was a priest and a prophet. He was the father of the great fighters, his sons; Kyobe Kyomubazzi, Mirimu, Mukasa and others.

The King explained what had taken them to Ssese and in Wannema's shrines. Wannema accepted to help the King and agreed to give the King his son Kyobe Kyomubazzi. Kyobe Kyomubazzi had spiritual powers known as Kibuuka. He had capacity to move on water and in air and he would disappear in oblivion and reappear. Other sons of Wannema decided to travel with the King back but Kyobe Kyomubazzi decided to go alone. At first the Kabaka had refused the offer because of the big price that was attached in taking

Kyobe Kyomubazzi in case he dies at the battle front. On accepting the conditions, the King was making a spiritual covenant with the priest Wannema.

Wannema and Ssekabaka Nnakibinge making a spiritual covenant

Some conditions were set for the King before taking Kyobe Kyomubazzi, Wannema's son;

• Surrendering a Prince in exchange for his son Kyobe Kyomubazzi.
• This condition was difficult for the Kabaka Nakibinge and after strong negotiations they agreed that the Kabaka should take Kyobe Kyomubazzi but the second condition was set;

• Returning the remains of Kyobe Kyomubazzi in case he dies at the battle front and also give Wannema the King's traditional symbolic and ritual twin known as "Omulongo wa Kabaka" which was the King's umbilical cord. In our culture so much is attached to one's umbilical cord. It is like owning someone's life. This therefore became a spiritual covenant.

Kabaka Nakibinge and his delegation left Ssese on the promise that Kyobe

Kyomubazzi was to join them later. However, they were surprised because on reaching the Lake shore on the other side Kyobe Kyomubazzi had already arrived and was waiting for them on the lake shores. From the lake shores they walked to the King's place and they were surprised that Kyobe Kyomubazzi had already arrived there and he was inspecting the King's military. The King was surprised on the nature of this fighter and how he made his movements. He named him Kibuuka which means somebody who can jump miles and miles. From that time Kyobe Kyomubazzi was named Kibuuka Omumbaale. The fighting was intense but Kibuuka used to fight in space in a dark cloud. From there he sent sharp spears and arrows and hails of fire and always wiped out the enemy. Finally they won the war. However, in the course of fighting he fell in love with a Munyoro girl called Nakayima who was so beautiful and on a sad note he told this girl all his secrets on how he fought in the clouds. The girl used this opportunity to alert the Banyoro soldiers on where Kibuuka used to hide.

During the fighting they sent many spears in the clouds above the fighters on the battle front and Kibuuka was finally killed. However, on falling, he fell in Mbaale in Mpigi in a big muvule tree.

When the battle ended, Nakibinge never fulfilled the conditions that were set for him by Wannema the Holy Priest and ever since when the Kingdom has unexplainable problems, those who know attribute it to the broken covenant. Therefore such covenants have been made on several occasions and they have been broken. This is dangerous because whenever such covenants are made God's spirit is in close observance and God is a witness himself.

THE SPRITUAL CONVENANT OF KABAKA KATO KINTU

The rule of Wasswa Bemba who was popularly known as Bemba Musota was so brutal and tyrannical to his people. Time came when even his people decided to desert him and hide in the forests to escape the tyranny. They were residing in the forests in temporary structures and they had no hope.

Much as Bemba's rule was like this, he was also adorned with spiritual powers though he used them in the wrong way. This required his brother to fight him using force of arms and finally he had to trek as far as Ethiopia and Egypt for training as earlier explained in this book.

In Egypt and Ethiopia he was given military and financial assistance and he was trained in war skills. He had to seek God's blessing to overthrow his brother Wasswa Bemba. He had to make spiritual covenants with the priests and prophets in the shrines on behalf of God to also get special powers. The first condition was to restore and to preserve the sanctuary of God (Ekitebe ky'obwakatonda).

The second condition was to put in place rule of law and to administer his people justly following the orders of God.

After winning the war he had to fulfill these two conditions. The ten years he spent in Egypt and Ethiopia on training, he had become keen on issues to do with the powers and orders of God. Failing to fulfill God's covenant is the source of all problems for mankind. It is like making an agreement with your wife, your child or any other person. God is always there in presence as a witness. Therefore, in order to avoid such problems it is important to keep God's covenant.

Kato Kintu on winning the war, he summoned the ruling council in Busujju on a hill known as Nnono to formulate laws on which society was to be governed and to fulfill the covenant he had made in the shrines in Egypt and Ethiopia. Many clan heads joined Buganda while others remained independent in their tribes. In this meeting they made a joint treaty that was to bring the rule of law to the people.

Kato reconstructed God's sanctuary and from that time this sanctuary was referred to as Akaalo ka Buganda - the sacred cultural village of Buganda. This sanctuary has been transferred from one place to another by the different kings. This was a great mistake of transferring it from one place to another. This is because the sanctuary is like God's eye and link and a plan of God that is not supposed to change. This sanctuary is supposed to be at Nnono. Kato Kintu was right because this sanctuary was given to our forefather Kintu Kitaka Nawansi Kyawadda and he left Akaalo ka Buganda at Nnono and that is where Kato Kintu left it. He constructed his palace at Magonga Hill. From that time all the traditional and cultural heritages of Buganda are called Nnono to mean the origin of tradition was at Nnono hill.

Generation after generation, Akaalo ka Buganda has been changed from place to another by various kings from Nnono to Kangulumira in Bugerere, to Ddindo in Maligita in Bugerere and the last place it was taken at Kaazi in Kyadondo. Our covenant with God has never changed. It started in a meeting called Ttabamawanga and was generally based on the following;

• Restoring and protecting the sanctuary of God.
• The rule of law to the people of Buganda which focuses on creating a just society where people are fairly administered according to the orders of God.
• Respecting the integrity of all stakeholders.

The Covenant of Akaalo ka Buganda made at Nnono goes as follows;

GOD'S CONVENANT BETWEEN KATO KINTU AND HIS PEOPLE

GLORY BE TO HIS HOLY NAME.
ALL NATIONS OF THE WORLD SHOULD PRAISE HIM
IN THEIR LANGUAGES. PEOPLE OF ALL NATIONS,
RACES AND LANGUAGES IN THE WORLD SHOULD
PRAISE HIM FOREVER, GENERATION AFTER GENER-
ATION. THE WONDERS OF HIS WORK DISPLAY THE
FIRMAMENT.
I, THE KABAKA WHO TAKES LEADERSHIP AND THE
MANTLE
WHO TAKES THESE INSTRUMENTS OF POWER TO
ADMINISTER BUGANDA AND
THE BAGANDA, THE GRAND SON OF MUWAWA,
THE DECENDAND OF THE HIGHEST GOD,
SWEAR IN THE NAME OF THE LIVING TO BEAR
TRUE ALLEGIENCE TO THE PEOPLE OF BUGANDA
TOGETHER WITH MY COUNCIL, THAT WE SHALL AT
ALL TIMES PRESERVE THIS CONVENANT OF NNONO
AND THAT WE SHALL USE IT AS LAW TO GOVERN
THE PEOPLE OF BUGANDA AND THE ENTIRE KING-
DOM, THE CLANS THE CLAN HEADS, THE NOBLES,
THE ROY-ALS, HEADS OF FAMILIES, LADIES, GENTLE-
MEN AND CHILDREN.

THAT WE SHALL DESIST FROM SHEDING BLOOD
FOR NO REASON. THE FEAR OF GOD AND TAKING
TROUBLE TO KNOW HIS WAYS AND GROLIFY HIS

NAME ALL THE TIME AS A CHOSEN RACE, FROM US ALL NATIONS RISE.

WE DO HERE BY ESTABLISH THE SANCTUARY OF GOD INCLUDING HIS HOLY SHRINES AS THE SOURCE OF ALL TRADITIONS AND OUR TRUE HERITAGE FOR OUR EDUCATION AND SOURCE OF ALL KNOWL-EDGE, A PLACE OF MEETING OF MINDS, A PLACE OF ENDOWMENT AND OUR CREATION AND KNOWING GOD WHO CREATED US.

THAT THIS COUNCIL OF CLAN HEADS MASENGERE AND ON BEHALF OF BUGAN-DA HERE AT NNONO, ALL COMBINED SHALL BE REFFERED TO AS BU-GANDA BUTUDDE AND THAT THEY SHALL TAKE FULL RESPONSIBILITY TO LEAD A JUST SOCIETY AS LAW ESTABLISHED AND THAT ALL THE PEOPLE OF BUGANDA SHALL FOLLOW THIS COVENANT FROM TODAY AND FOR FUTURE GENERATION SHALL TAKE OUR CULTURE, BELIEF, CLANS, NORMS INTENDED TO BRING SANITY AND GOOD MORALS IN OUR SOCIETY BY OBSERVING DISCPLINED CON-DUCT AND THAT PEOPLE

SHALL TAKE FORGIVENESS, RESPECT, ESTABLISHED INSITITUTIONS OF LEADERSHIPAPPOINTED AND NOMINATED, CREATIVITY, FORECASTING, HEALTH, FAIR JUSTICE, HARD WORK, ARCHTECTURAL SKILLS AND THE 52 CLANS AS THE SUPREME LAW.

THAT UNLESS OTHERWISE PEOPLE SHALL TAKE TROUBLE TO KNOW THEIR ROOTS, TO BE FAITHFUL

TO ONE ANOTHER, TO RESPECT PUBLIC PROPERTY
AND CARRY OUT COMMUNAL WORK AND AT ALL
TIME PROTECT THE ENVIRON-MENT THROGH THE
ESTABLISHED NORMS AND VALUES. THAT OUR PEO-
PLE SHALL OBSERVE THE ESTABLISHED LEADERSHIP
STRUC-TURES FROM THE KING, PRIME MINISTER,
AND HEADS OF CLANS AND THAT WE SHALL RE-
SPECT ALL THE RELIGIOUS INSITITUTIONS ESTAB-
LISHED FOR THIS PURPOSE.
AND THAT AT ALL TIMES WE SHALL STRIVE AT ALL
TIMES TO PRESRVE OUR NATION WHILE OBSERVING
THE CORE VALUES OF UNITY, RECONCILIATION AND
LOVE FOR ONE ANOTHER.

This covenant was written on animal skins and in pictures and photo-graphic impression. Rituals were performed and the spirit of God descended on those who were present; that is the Kabaka, priests, prophets and clan heads and they spoke in strange tongues. They worshipped and glorified God. The second copy of the Covenant was written on stones and the spirit was asked to write it on the hearts of the Baganda and the Holy Spirit accepted. From this time this Covenant came to be known as the Nnono Covenant, meant to keep Buganda intact.

5

THE SPIRIT AND THE SPIRITUAL WORLD

Many times everywhere and all the time, people talk about the word, "Spirit". What is meant by the word sprit or ghost? The Spirit is Godly and the spirit relates to Godly power. The spirit is the energy form for every living kind. The Spirit is one True God; from the True God to God the Creator; from God the Creator to the Holy Spirit. The spirit is the first and the last the omnipotent and the omnipresent.

Photo demonstrating the power of the Holy Spirit that spreads to the entire universe

The embodiment of the Spirit is the Holy Spirit (Mwoyo Kitiibwa) from which all forms of Spirits and spiritual variations or hubs are derived and names given accordingly to suit the purpose. These spiritual forms can be categorized into four branches;

MUKASA

On the side of life the body spirit is known as Mukasa. Mukasa is the spiritual part in charge of the air that we breathe, so the source of life and the water that gives life. This is the soul form that stays with the physical being of any living forms to enable them utilize the stored life so to facilitate life. There

56

is stored life in cells such as seeds, semen, in the air we breathe, in the water we drink, in the food we eat and in every other aspect of life, and so Mukasa the angel and Ministry are in-charge of that jurisdiction. The soul of Mukasa lives in the space of the universe, in air, on landscapes, in lakes and rivers. It manifests its self in living creatures and in the dew and the rain. Mukasa is the SPIRIT or the store of life from which all living creatures derive life.

MUSOKE

Musoke is the spirit or ghost of understanding and all human races have it and it is represented in the symbol of the rainbow. Literary it means; "First, understand the Lord your God"; in Luganda "Musooke Mutegeere Katonda wammwe"; that God is the beginning of everything. Has no beginning and will have no end. THIS IS AN IMPORTANT COMMANDEMENT. This spirit helps our consciousness to judge the right and the wrong in our daily lives. It is the guide of all human understanding. It is called the SENSE.

The spirit is represented in the rainbow and that is how it manifests itself. The seven colors of the rainbow remind the people of the ten commandments of God given to the human race. The seven colors are the seven commandments and the remaining three are hidden by God from us. They are omnipotent. The remaining three commandments are hidden in the Trinity of God that is; the Most High God, God the Creator, and God the Holy Spirit. The seven are the manifestations of God's creation that displays the firmament as God wishes.

When this Sense part descends to the earth, it works hand in hand with the other two spirits Mukasa (Spirit part i.e. stored life) and Kiwanuka (Power part) to make the Trinity of the Holy Spirit. All other spirits hail from Trinity of the Holy Spirit mentioned above, or to perform God's work among the people he created, in following God's will, giving people God's messages, wisdom and understanding and supplying people with their needs on behalf of God.

LUBAALE

The spirit that lives in all creatures is known as Lubaale, meaning permanence. This is known as the everlasting life or life eternal in every creature. God's ignition of life! This spirit is omnipresent and guides all creatures on the entire universe. It is the spirit called LIFE. The best example is a snail that has water in all weather conditions. Even human beings survive in all areas be it a desert or the very cold areas. The sustenance or nourishment of life is entirely God's will and that is Lubaale (Eternity or the ignition of life) whereas Mukasa is stored life in any form.

On the other hand, this spirit called Lubaale helps all creatures to get messages from God or to communicate with God directly meaning that everybody or organ, spiritual or physical is each other's watchman on behalf of God. This enables God to get the exact without going through mediums. The life part is like a magnet. It is like a radio or telephone telecommunication using waves and channels to send messages to people. This spirit lives in all creatures including those that are microscopic. That is why even plants have forces that enable them to look for light or water to enable them, grow properly.

THE HIDDEN SECRET IN LUBAALE SPIRIT

The Life Spirit says that, "Souls have been sent to work on the earth but do they know the purpose of God and the purpose of spirits? This is a mockery. I will never forgive any creature much as you are made to believe that you are people of God's creation. I am ready to destroy all the sinners. They should not owe life on my behalf. Are living creatures aware that they owe their survival to me? Who will understand this when they have bad hearts? The storm is coming, diseases will attack them, many wars and many other atrocities are coming. Many of them are defying my power posing as God on earth. Cursed are they. I am omnipresent and am seeing all. I will not allow them to use their bodies to despise me and my messengers. I will not allow them destroy my great works and wonders. That is out and to hell with it".

THE GHOST
OMUZIMU

Photo showing a ghost/spirit coming out of a human being

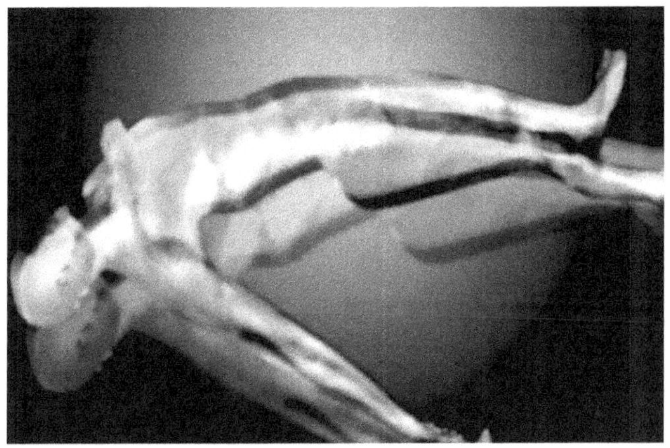

The Ghost spirit or the human spirit is called Omuzimu in Luganda. All human beings have this spirit called the consciousness of the heart or the inner man. When a person dies, this spirit can manifest its self among human beings and sometimes causes people to get dreams or to see it in dreams. The dead are called the late. When his spirit manifests itself it is called omuzimu, meaning the spirit that comes back and manifests itself among human beings literary known as Omuzzi mu Bantu (meaning the returnee spirit) abbreviated as Omuzimu. This is the part some witchdoctors manipulate using evil spirits to manifest themselves through incarnation to disorganize your inner man and communication between you and your God. To have this link rehabilitated is actually very difficult and if unlucky can put you on the verge of death.

Painting showing human spirit

There is an assembly of the soul, where the soul is prepared before it is put into a living being. There is transference of the soul into the physical being. In episode of assembly of the soul, to take its complete form, this is what happens; The three spirits; Mukasa (Body Spirit) which composes of stored life i.e. spirit, Musoke which is the sense full part and Lubaale which has the eternal life are collected and put into a carrier, call it a container or vehicle to form an "Inner Man" referred to as the Ghost which in full is "God's command" meaning, "GO SIT ON" on such and such living form as desired or seen fit. The fifth composition and interesting part of the soul is that of Satan. This add-on rule acts as a spy and provides intelligence on whatever you are up to, because he is also a spirit.

THE SPIRIT IN TOTALITY

All living creatures are embedded with the spirit including plants, animals and human beings. Sometimes you may admire another person or you may be thinking about someone and his or her spirit reveals the secret to that person or that person gets to know of it, even when you have not communicated to each other.

The spirit works like a telecommunication. You may pick a stone to throw it towards a bird facing the other side and it flies away before you even throw the stone towards it. Someone may not be holy in his ways and someone tells you that he or she is not a good person yet they have never interacted. Who reveals this? It is the spirit.

The spirit causes people to have dreams, to get visions and to forecast what will happen in the future. The spirit may talk to you as an individual, can make you laugh or cry. That is why people say the spirit talked to me or say my spirit made me think about that person.

At times mankind refers to it to as parenting spirit and keeper for man-kind. It manifests itself in the sky like an animal or in form of a person and it destroys property like houses. That is why sometimes people who are aware of the works of the spirits and pay much attention to fall of ice stones, dew and the rain. They usually celebrate with drums, harps, organs and sometimes offer prayers to God.

In God's creation, Spirit means the Trinity, which is; the Most High God, God the Creator and God the Holy Ghost or Spirit. The sources of life, the source of wisdom, master of death, source of all blessings, source of knowledge and all human understanding, master of land, master of heaven, life for all life, giver of life to plants and animals, the beginning and the end, the covenant, the word, the voice of life and fire, the creator of heavens and earth, the omnipresent, the omnipotent and the Most High God.

Nothing was made without Him. Life and death are all in his powers. This means the power of creation is manifested among human beings but people interpret it differently. This explains why there are many religions because people are confused when it comes to understanding the works and operations of the Most High God.

God made the spirit His covenant with the earth. God hid Himself in the Outer Planet and His spirit entered into all living creatures. That is why our consciousness tells us what is right and what is wrong. Then He also sent His messengers to remind people, to counsel and guide them, to treat them and to give them medicine and how to identify the different diseases.

God's religion is embedded in cultural norms and values. Even when you pretend not to see this, the wonders of God on the earth will show you this. The covenant became God's manifestation to man. All God's power is manifested in living creatures but boasting is the problem which makes, people think that they are greater than God. Some people do not believe in the presence of God. Others believe in Him, however, they do not accept his messengers. Other people create an impression that God belongs to them alone and they monopolize Him. They think that, the way they understand him should be the way all people on earth should understand Him. Sometimes material benefits make people boast around, despise others, attack other religions, steal, kill others, yet the Spirit sees everything. Whatever you think and do, you will never get satisfied and when you die you go empty handed! Many times this leads to self-destruction.

The world and its fullness belong to God because all things were made by Him. He is the creator, the Most High who uses His power of the Spirit.

This power is embedded in every living creature according to how much he measured this power to every creature, according to their types. In totality, they perform God's work. The Spirits guide creatures of all types to work as God's army to put right, to teach and to destroy where necessary as it has been in the past generations. God has been doing like that, generation after generation using his own methods of putting the wrongs right.

Putting right was the very method God used while destroying the Dinasours that were destroying the environment and encroaching on human peace. This happened four billion years ago. God destroyed them using His Spirit through Thunder known as Nnende meaning boss in Luganda, and that was their end. This is how God has been working generation after generation.

Painting showing how God used Thunder to destroy the Dinosaurs

THE DEMANDS OF THE SPIRIT

The covenant of the Spirit is that every state should have the holy places as a sanctuary of the Spirit of God. From such places, the clans and lineages get wisdom and understanding of God and from which people get communication messages from God.

The history of our country from the beginning was having such sanctuaries of God and these were the places of covenant of people with God. Such places were known as Akaalo ka Buganda (Buganda's Sacred Village. To the messengers of God, this was always the headquarters of God's presence. It was the meeting place for all the clans and lineages. People filled with the Spirit of the Lord were put in charge of such places. The prophets and priests were in position to safeguard the places and were able to know God's messages to the people. They were able to interpret God's plans to the people and the works of the spirit. They listened to them, used them and assisted the world to avoid destruction because of its evil deeds done out of ignorance. The spirit has been descending upon us and has been giving us messages through people. But the world is disobedient because of evil gatherings, fear, being hard hearted, being greedy and liars. For how long will the people continue in disbelief?

Look at your environment and its surroundings, your language, your colour / race, your talent, your blessing, your origin and ancestry, you're thinking and view, your dreams and the messages always said. You will understand, think ahead, wake up and follow the right path and stop suffering in this evil world.

DEATH

Death is the cessation of all biological functions that sustain a living organism. For human beings, it is a transformation into another state. In Luganda death (Okufa) is derived from a verb okufuula (change of form). Therefore death is a change of form. If human beings are still alive they are given names (Okutuumwa) which means that person is a messenger of God (Omutume in Luganda)

When a person dies, it is said that he/she has changed form (afudde embeera) from the flesh or bodily state to a spiritual state. When he/she dies, they call him or her the late or "the departed" (omugenzi). If he or she is not yet buried, he/she is referred to as a dead body (Omufu) who has transformed himself or herself (eyeefudde).Because he or she has gone, they call him the late (omugenzi). If he or she manifests himself or her self-gain and appears in a spirit form, they call him or her ghost or returnee spirit (Omuzzi mu Bantu), meaning coming back to manifest himself or herself again to people. Death occurs in very many ways. There is a natural death which is mandatory for all people. There is also intentional and unintentional death, which occurs as a result of terminal illness or sickness, or as a result of murder. People die after committing suicide, excessive alcoholism or sometimes, according to God's will.

Intentional death can occur as a result of drug abuse or excessive alcoholism. With this, people refer to the person as having died long time ago because all along he has been waiting for his time to die as the drugs made him weak, slim, and generally weakened his or her life. People begin to wonder, why somebody who has over compromised their life due to excesses, would fall short of an immediate burial!

If death is non-intentional like an accident, a person can wither like a flower, or go into comma or just die abruptly. The 'ghost person' moves out of the person first and then followed by the Life Spirit (Lubaale). This marks the end of life of the flesh.

The spirit is the power of God or God's will in the living organism. Life is the air we breathe or the heartbeat, call it the pulse. The inner person is the human spirit or soul created by God in the beginning of time. All spirits were created at once in the beginning for all creatures including animals, birds and insects. These were given a limited life span. Life spans are different. They are varied according God's plan. The life of angels is different from that of aliens or human beings and so on and so forth.

However, the death we are talking about is for human beings. When a person dies, the spirit comes out of him or her. The person's spirit is com-posed of four parts: The Spirit of God, the spirit of the body, the spirit of life and the spirit of purpose.

The spirit of body is when someone dies and is buried. The part of the soul or the spirit that remains with body is the spirit of the body known as body spirit or Mukasa to look after the body and interests of the deceased partic-ularly his or her lineage. It also plays a caretaker role when someone dies and goes into the divine world for further instructions and returns to kick start off from where he or she had stopped.

The spiritual part of the soul or spirit is called Lubaale that has eternal life and enables all living creatures to have direct communication with God. This spirit works as a channel for everything that you do on earth. Because it is the spiritual part of the soul, it records every activity of every living being. It gives life and that is why without it there is no life. When a living being ceases, this part is the first one to reach heaven so that captured data can be downloaded. That is how complicated it is! Satan (Olukokobe) lives in the human soul and works as a spy. Whatever you do is reported to the Spiritual soul called Lubaale including your future plans so that all can be recorded. All your information is sent to God including images such that on the Day of Judgment you cannot deny anything!

The Godly Spirit is that of the Sense Spirit. The fear of the Lord is where knowledge and wisdom start from. It oscillates in space when a person dies, between the divine world and the earthly world as a link between the body and the divine world. Being a sense spirit from the sense ministry of God, the orders and commands of God or the spiritual instructions are conveyed to it. At the same time it plays a supportive role towards the spirit that stays with the body, in helping to convey information so as to put interests and desires to effect, since the body spirit has to fulfill its roles such as taking care of its lineage. That is why people say that the dead can see and hear. This explains why the possessions or wealth left by the dead is durable! This part is called Musoke.

The human or messianic spirit is that person that was sent to fulfill purpose on earth or elsewhere by using the talents and gifts that were adorned upon him or her so as to do the needful. Therefore, the human spirit is God's messenger who is judged upon conduct on return to heaven. This part goes back upon lapse of duties that is death, for judgment with the spiritual part which has the recordings while on earth. According to God's judgment, this part is either kept in the sanctuary of spirits or it is burnt due to poor conduct or it is sent back on earth to spread God's work. This is also called a wondering spirit (Empewozimu).

The human spirit stays in heaven in the spiritual sanctuary until when it is returned. When it returns and there is no body to go into, it is what people refer to as the Ghost. When it returns when its body is still around, it is what they call 'resurrection'. When it returns into a body of another person like a young child, it is what they call 'being born again'. The child starts acting and behaving like the deceased in mind and conduct. This is called regeneration! When a person is born again or regenerated, he or she begins from where he or she stopped in the first life and promotes the new orders got from heaven and works with new methods depending on the way he or she has found the earth.

ARRANGEMENT OF THE SOUL UPON DEATH
BODY SPIRIT

BODY SPIRIT	*Referred to as Mukasa *Stays with the body *Looks after its lineage as a caretaker
GODLY SPIRIT	*Referred to as Musoke *Stays in space as a link between Heaven and Earth *Does God's work and gives support to the body spirit
HUMAN SPIRIT	*Referred to as Omuzimu (Ghost) or Inner man *Human Soul that goes back for judgment *It's act as carrier for all other parts before Death
SPIRITUAL SOUL	*Referred to as Lubaale meaning permanence *It does all recordings on behalf of God *Spiritual because it is derived from the Holy Spirit but works independently to give *God a direct account on all things.

The spirit may return to its people or relatives and find them in a state of disobedience when they need to be punished or when they have even sold the graveyard. The spirit may return when a child is demanding to be renamed after a person who died. It may also return when there is need to construct a temple or a shrine for God and need for worship. When you do not do this it becomes an issue, and he or she mobilizes other spirits and messengers that: These are the people who destroyed Buganda kingdom, these are the people who destroyed the fabric of clans!

These are the people who destroyed the social fabric of families!
Destroy them, reject them, and chase them away!

This means the spirit of the dead is annoyed, yet is a reporter of that issue, he or she is the prosecutor and at the same time the judge. Therefore you cannot win that case because you are totally ignorant about the issue as you did not exist at that time.

The human spirit may cause people to get dreams or may perform many other signs with other wondering spirits. Therefore I urge you not to despise the spirits of the dead persons (emizimu) pretending to cast them out. The spirits of animals that persecute people are the ones that are cast out.
They do not cast out the soul, or auxiliary spirits or ghosts without knowing purpose, or else you may cast yourself out.

Do not pretend to be so holy yet you are despising God's power. Do not engage in things you do not understand or else you risk death to join the spiritual world. God's spirits (the ghost), Lubaale and the helping spirits and angels must be respected. It is important to distinguish evil spirits from God's spirits. God's plans should be handled with a lot of care.

WHAT HAPPENS IN HEAVEN

On reaching into heaven all are assembled into a big hall full of excessive heat like that of a full blast oven, which some people call Purgatory or Ggapuka-tooli in some other languages. The purpose is to purity the spiritual person or soul free from all the human flesh contamination. This is where there is a lot of suffering and crying. Every person irrespective of socio-economic status starts at this place. It is from this place that you are taken into the presence of God's Spirit called Mwene (Overall Angel) to answer several questions according to your deeds on earth so as to deter-mine whether you are to go back to the earth or you are to remain in the place of suffering or you are to go into heaven.

The purgatory is a very big building as wide as from Uganda to South Africa! It is an outsized dome having two path ways; a wider one and a narrow one. Those who are expected to return are made to pass through the narrow way, while those expected to stay are made to pass through the wider way.
God's angel and four army officers pick you up with a single finger on their hands using power similar to magnetic force. Then you are brought to the door way depending on their plan.

On that day, on your way out you meet one of your great grandparents or an elder from your lineage that was made holy in heaven. The escorts or guards are very tall and dressed like the pharaoh's guards. By imagination, a tall or medium sized person ends at the soles of their boots! They hold big batons and swords. They have bright eyes like car spotlights.

Your great grandparent appears in the image of a real person, soft spoken and well conversant with Luganda or your local dialect. In his or her presence, he or she asks you, "Is God still watching over your life? That is his nature. Now let's go and meet God's Spirit and give your account. I am your intercessor. Do not fear my grandchild". He advises you whether you are to return to the earth or to stay in heaven or you're in imminent danger because of your bad ways.

The four tall huge men lead you outside. As you are heading to the court, you are joined by archangels. On the way you meet people dressed like nuns in white linen and with wings. When you reach into God's court you find huge men with big eyes. Then they bring a satellite and video to see all that you have been doing in life. After seeing all this you, are already aware of what is going to happen next depending on what you did while you were here on earth.

Inside, there is a setting of a court. God's spirit sits on the throne of judgment. You are taken in the courtyard and told everything. At this place you do not utter out any word. Your grandparent pleads for you and asks the Spirit of God to allow you go back on earth and put your record in order. Then judgment is given. There is also a gallery with people you know and those you do not know. By this time they are already aware of God's judgment through invisible public address systems.

Outside this place, is where you are made to see the star, which is, further up in a distance. It is a big red sun but very far from where you are standing. It is wider in perspective with sounds of thunder. That is the heaven where God dwells. Below it is a place of worship (Eggulumizo). Nobody reaches where God dwells because God is hidden. The world is led by the Trinity of Musoke (Sense), Mukasa (Stored Life i.e. Spirit) and Kiwanuka (Force) as we saw in the previous chapter.

God is praised by his creation from grass, trees, heavens and the earth, the dew and rain. The difference is that you may not walk normally but you may fly from one place to another. People in their spiritual form consume milky like clouds that are sweeter than milk. What happens in heaven are prayers, praising, singing, offering on alters, and praising God with pipe organs. Even in the forests there is nothing but praising God. The grass sings lovely melodies such as; Hosanna! Hosanna!

There are mansions and a lot of games. Mansions and roads are made of precious glittering stones that cannot be compared to anything on earth. All is made of marble, silver, gold and gems. You also see people seated on the verandah of these mansions.

What is scaring is the burning furnace to destroy evil spirits of those who are engaged in destroying God's creation especially the environment. Their dust is thrown in a very big valley covered with darkness. In it there is a dark evil forest.

What we see on earth also exists in heaven for example lakes, strips and straights, forests, big cities, big armies dressed in white clothes and many more. Everything in heaven praises God. Luganda language is spoken widely. People meant to return to the earth are taken into a training center and they are trained in God's ways such as love for one another and forgiveness. They are trained to avoid being greedy, to avoid theft, adultery, hurting others and putting them at loss. They are taught repentance, avoiding evil and are taught to respect their cultural norms and values and the environment according to God's will.

People supposed to return are escorted by angels dressed in white for a short distance. They leave you to continue with your journey and they return. Some go left while others go right and others descend directly to the earth depending on where you are going. This takes place in a blink of an eye.

In heaven there are places like those you see here on earth. There are settlements for God's prophets and messengers (Balubaale). Because of the many dwelling places, many spirits of God that do the judgment trans-form themselves accordingly. Some of God's spirits are women. Remember God is hidden and cannot be seen. There is no religion in heaven. They just examine the gifts of the Spirit and the good deeds that are in the individual.

6

THE THREE DOCTRINES AND DIMENSIONS IN GOD'S CREATION

SATAN (Olukokobe)

Satan (Olukokobe) is also an angel coming directly from God as Spirit. Satan also came with other messengers such as the "Shadow of Death Angel". In our native language is known as Walumbe meaning "Spiritual Devil". Satan gives the Spiritual Devil roles particularly those to do with inflicting pain and causing death. God in his creation gives roles and He does not take it away because He keeps His covenant. Even on Satan it is the same story. Satan was given responsibilities much as he became disobedient, God could not take away the responsibilities from him. God instead decided to guide Satan by revising his terms of reference with emphasis on detective work.

God gave Satan more responsibilities and made him his right hand man to perform his duties instead of keeping him on opposition. The responsibilities were maintained but had to implement God's orders. He was supposed to give God information and the roles performed are from God. God linked Satan to His other messengers and other departments, but he is supposed to work independently with his angels but using God's powers.

Satan started working and performing his roles while communicating directly with God, according to God's plan because creation was done once and was fixed. Satan's power was outright. God gave Satan powers to spy all living creatures, to kill and to destroy. Satan was given powers to dwell in people's souls and all living creatures. Satan has effectively performed these duties only that the world is not aware.

Satan's spirit works hand in hand with other spirits in constituting souls that is; Mukasa the spirit of stored life, Musoke the spirit of sense and Lubaale the spirit of Eternal Life and the Ghost or human spirit which acts as a carrier for other spirits. The human spirit is what is referred to as a ghost or returnee spirit upon death of a person or any other living creature. Satan becomes the fifth spirit upon composition of a living creature. Satan is God's spy in creation. Satan is God's spirit representing him on earth. That is why sometimes when it comes to sinners people say that, that person will be punished by the world. Or they say the world is round he or she will see. This is because the role of Satan is to covertly kill and destroy.

The difference is that Satan in his nature from creation is swift. As other spirits of God were planning to undertake a duty, Satan would go ahead with his own plan, deviating from the plans of others. The way Satan operates does not want organized plans. He always disorganized meetings of the spirits with God. As spirits were planning to do this, Satan would do the opposite. That is why even in our daily lives, the spirit of Satan stifles people's morale. As the other spirits were planning something, Sa-tan begun posing questions like, "will you manage?" "Aren't you toiling in vain?" "Will people like what you are doing?" "Who will take that positive?" "Won't people laugh at you?" "Is it useful?" "Why don't you leave it?" "But where do you get the knowledge you use in your daily lives?" "Why do you pretend to be wiser than God?" "You boast around! Let's watch and see if at all it will work out!"

Painting showing the Council of Spirits

From Left to Right Hand Olukokobe (Satan), Mukasa, Lubaale, Musoke and the Inner man in the spiritual world

When other spirits saw that Satan was disorganizing them and disorganizing their work by always doing the contrary, because his role was that of a spy and disorganizing in order to evoke reaction, all meetings they fell apart.

The other spirits that comprised of the Council; Musoke the Sense Spirit, Mukasa the Spirit of stored life or body spirit, Lubaale the Life Spirit and the Inner man or Human Spirit complained to God. God ordered Satan to descend onto the earth and perform his duties there. He was ordered to spy all other spirits and give God information. God in return would pay Satan for his work.

When Satan reached here on earth he captured all the other spirits on earth and its fullness; spying them and disorganizing them by giving false information, giving wrong doers petty gifts, using evil powers and put-ting in people bad hearts. The world became disorganized because Satan started making himself God, started killing people, destroying the environment while spying, hence disorganizing God's plan on earth. This has been done generation after generation putting every creature at risk.

Satan was given a commander who was the Spiritual Devil known as Walumbe or the Angel of Death. Walumbe came with active messengers. Satan started ruling over many things of God's creation such as the Dead Sea, active volcano, deserts and others. The Dead Sea has no living creatures. Satan fell in the Dead Sea and then his deputizing angel, the Spiritual Devil i.e. Walumbe, attacked the Black Race to make them suffer and then other spirits of the Spiritual Devil spread to different parts of the world to cause anarchy. When Satan was descending to the earth, rage, fire, storm and earthquake followed him. That power entered into the Dead Sea and it became dead instantly and destroyed all the life in it. It became a lake of salt and ash and many other things that are not known.

The Dead Sea is a liability because it emits bad gases; its water is dirty and contaminated. It spreads diseases and spiritual degeneration to who-ever goes near it. However it is an asset because people get salt from it, it is used for recreation, attracts tourists and helps the country when it comes to getting foreign exchange.

Map of the Dead Sea

Courtesy Photo

KAYIUK

After all that happening, God realized that the earth was suffering, Satan, had become a problem. He was spying; killing, destroying and people were going through a lot of hardship. God in his mercy decided to liberate the earth and mankind. He sent his messenger Kayiuk to liberate it from Satan and the Spiritual Devil to enable people return to God and allow God's power to rule the earth again.

Kayiuk came as the first prophet of God to save the earth and guide it on what to do. On top of this he was to enforce good acts and guide mankind on how to avoid evil. Kayiuk landed in Egypt with a big and strong army in different aspects. The army was composed of Aliens and messengers like Kayiikuuzi. In the black race, God sent Kayiikuuzi. However by the time Kayiuk was sent, Satan and the Spiritual Devil had overshadowed the whole earth.

Kayiuk was a liberator. He came from the Spirit of Musoke —a spirit of liberation, generation after generation up to the present day. This is how God has been working through sending us messengers to save us much as mankind is very difficult.

However, Kayiikuuzi was a great friend of Walumbe. He chased him in vain while he was laughing at him, hiding under ground then coming back on the surface. It became a game of hide and seeks. Satan helped the Spiritual Devil greatly and they defeated Kayiuk and Kayiikuuzi.

Kayiuk fought tirelessly but other departments outnumbered his army because Satan had a powerful spy network. Kayiuk went back and reported back to God that he had failed to perform the task of fighting Satan and the Angel of Shadow of Death i.e. Spiritual Devil known as Walumbe.

What God did was to change his work ways and commanded to stop the fighting. Instead he ordered for negotiation to streamline roles. Therefore Kayiuk's role of capturing Satan and Walumbe plus other spirits were put to halt. This was done amicably without resorting to war.

They brought a judge or an arbitrator called Nnende. Nnende guided the negotiations on behalf of God as it was in the beginning in the event of fighting. The Attorney General Angel (Nnende) ruled that every spirit should form its own army and work methodologies, and so it was. It therefore became God's plan that was agreed upon.

The problem was that nobody willing to accept defeat as both parties were warriors. All of them wanted to rule the earth. It is Nnende who made a fair judgment to end the wars, disobedience and ignorance, in addition to guiding the entire spiritual world and the people. The commandments to bring about order and to share power amicably and peacefully, instead of role conflict were formulated.

NNENDE

After Nnende had solved this crisis as a judge and after bringing about peace, because of ignorance people became indebted yet Nnende the Attorney General or Judge Angel, worked on behalf of God to solve the whole issue. He summarized it in one thing known as God's Sanctuaries; in Buganda it is the Sacred Village or Akaalo ka Buganda to act as the headquarter of God's presence. The aim was to enable God's kingdom come to the earth and to enable His will be done on earth as it is in heaven. To do this, he had to humble himself to come and be born in the human flesh. Through our lineage he became a liberator in order to save the sinful world.

He became human and lived with us. He left everything and died to put up sanctuaries of God to save the world from destruction and to please God. After this, he was to repossess his honor as a Judge in the kingdom of God in heaven and on earth. That is why he came up with an arrangement to save the world from destruction. The Sacred village here in Buganda (Akaalo ka Buganda) is the solution and elsewhere in other Sanctuaries. That is where our liberation lies and it and that is where God's plan to put the world into order lies.

GOD'S DOCTRINE AND DIMENSION OF CREATION

The world should know that that every creature was created by God who is a merciful God. He becomes angry to the sinners and those who are disobedient. God wants the whole earth to be happy and to live in peace to praise him and his holy name and to sanctify him. Satan takes the sinners, the disobedient and those who boast around into temptation. However when you repent to God Satan leaves you alone. When you fail to decide to follow God's ways and you are taken up by evil, Satan will lead you into temptation and then report you to God or completely destroy you.

This has two interpretations; Kayikuuzi is a messenger and prophet of God. These are the messages given to people always to warn the world and bring about security. Such messages are given to clan heads (Abataka), heads of shrines and palaces headed by the head of clan heads, who is the king of Buganda or Ssaabataka at the top. Sometimes Ssaabataka delegates some duties to his Prime minister (Katikkiro). What unites all these is the Sacred Village (Akaalo ka Buganda) to fulfill God's plan for the world, to receive God's help, to get peace, and to receive long life from God, and to be sanctified forever. This Sacred Village must be put in place.

7

THE SANCTUARY OF GOD, THE SACRED CULTURAL VILLAGE -AKAALO KA BUGANDA AMATENDO

After the overthrow and downfall of Kabaka Bemba Musota, a tyrant, all tribes and nations were summoned in a council and sat to agree on the right system and democratic principles on which society was to be governed. The principles on which society was to be governed had to be in line with the covenant that Kabaka Kato Kintu I had made in the holy shrines with the angels and spiritual prophets in Egypt and Ethiopia in the rituals of worship that were performed to dedicate him to God. It is in these two countries that Kabaka Kato Kintu I raised a spiritual case to the divine world against his twin brother Wasswa Bemba Musota who was using God's power in a way that was unacceptable. He was mistreating people of God and disorganizing and dishonoring the chosen race of God which is Buganda.

Many different nations after the war gathered and formulated just principles that were to bring peace and unity. Some tribes joined Buganda and became clans while others remained independent in their integrities though they maintained the diplomatic relations with Buganda. This is why you find out that though states in our region are independent, they share so many things in common such as languages, language usage, cultural beliefs, mode of worship, dress code, type of music and dance, agricultural practices, crops grown, royal regalia and systems of administration.

These fair play principles were intended to bring transformations in their states with an aim of bringing peace and stability among God's people. It took them ten years, to formulate these principles that were preserved as heritages in norms, values and cultures. This was ample time for them to sort out all issues so as to bring good governance and a just society in the sub-region.

81

This arrangement was the source of all heritages, norms, values, cultures and traditions, institutions of kingship, clan heads, royal councils, elderly councils, youth councils and good ways of life and practices.

The formulated system and good practice of the national conference was established and the meeting was referred as Ttabamawanga, which literary means the Council of Nations. This place where the Council of Nations sat was God's sanctuary known as Akaalo ka Buganda – the sacred cultural village or Akaalo Amatendo aka Buganda. It is this village that became the nucleus of Buganda's heritage for clans, cultures and traditions. This nucleus of heritage even became the center for the operations of the Trinity of God's Leadership manifestation.

Ssekabaka Kato Kintu I built his palace and city on Magonga Hill, on the next hill to the Sacred Village, in Busujju County. He made Nnono Hill a center for all clans. The clans established their administrative units, and every clan was able to get a secretariat and a meeting place for sorting out issues within the clans. Nnono therefore became a meeting place for all the clan heads or clan lords (Abataka) and ruling council (Abakungu) who used to sit and come up with strategies of promoting nationalism and patriotism among the Baganda which was referred to as Omwoyo gwa Buganda Ogutafa, meaning "One Spirit". Such patriotism helped to promote peace, unity, love for one another and good diplomatic relations. This was in respect of God's covenant with his people.

The above meetings became the source of Buganda's ruling council known as Olukiiko lwa Buganda or the ruling council. Another advisory council known as Ttaala – Meaning Light for the priests (Bakabona and Bassenkulu Council) was established. Another council was referred to as Masengere (Heads of Clans Council or the Abataka's Council) and the Youth Council (Olukiiko lw'Abazzukulu ba Buganda). All these councils operated on two offices; the Sanctuary of God or Akaalo ka Buganda and the institution of

Kingship (Obwakabaka). From these, many offices were created up to the village level to bring services nearer to the people. This became law.

From that time, the King's palace was separated from Akaalo ka Buganda so as to separate the administration of God from that of the Kabaka (King) and his agents. The King's palace was established at Magonga in Busujju and Akaalo ka Buganda, as it was during the reign of Kintu Kita-ka Nawansi Kyawadda, at Nnono Hill, though this time it was sanctified and dedicated to God and the security was increased.

THE ARRANGEMENT OF GOD'S SANCTUARY (AKAALO KA BUGANDA) ARMS OF LEADERSHIP IN BUGANDA KINGDOM

GOD'S ARM	1. CLAN TEMPLES
	2. GOD'S SANCTUARY OR HOLY SITE
	3. SPIRITUAL COUNSEL I.E. KATEBE

STATE ARM	1. EXECUTIVE (OLUKIIKO LWA BUGANDA)
	2. HOUSE OF LORDS (MASENGERE)
	3. SPIRITUAL COUNCIL (TAALA)
	4. CITZENS COUNCIL (ABAZZUKULU)

These are four councils; the Council of Lords (Olukiiko lwa Abataka or Masengere), the Council of Messengers of God (Olukiiko lwa Ttaala), the Executive (Olukiiko lwa Bakungu oba Buganda) and the Council of Citizens (Olukiiko lwa Bazzukulu ba Buganda. The councils played administrative and advisory roles in the Kingdom. These councils performed Buganda's duties and the administration was streamlined and peace prevailed. Kato Kintu I's administration was that of peace and unity. People viewed him as the shadow of God or "Ekisiikirize kya Katonda" and he became a King of fundamental change and transformation. He is one of the most celebrated Kings among all Kings of Buganda. It is him who established the ruling dynasty of Buganda including his Majesty Ronald Muwenda Mutebi Kimera II.

During the administration of Kato Kintu I, the Baganda strived as much as possible to keep God's covenant of Nnono. Even the Kings who followed Kato Kintu respected this covenant, and Buganda was a very powerful kingdom that defeated all her enemies. This is because the administration of man worked hand in hand with that of God at his sanctuary or Akaalo ka Buganda as the leadership had fewer slip-ups.

THE SPIRITUAL LIBERATION OF KABAKA KATO KINTU I

Some states for so long have been disintegrated and disorganized be-cause of ignorance, having few people with expertise, failure to preserve cultural institutions and heritage, wars, diseases, despising God's power or bad luck or a combination of all of them. Some kingdoms disintegrate but the sanctuaries of God remain intact like that of the Ethiopian Empire. There are some kingdoms that exist when the sanctuaries have perished or destroyed! This is not a good situation for the survival of the kingdom. Everything is done with a lot of difficulty in the kingdom and God considers less the prayers of the peoples of that kingdom. He treats them with despise. People in the kingdom are disorganized, their businesses are disorganized, they do not succeed in whatever they do, their first class citizens status is eroded steadily and they do not find God's favor even in the slightest of things. Knowledge and wisdom become something of the past.

The sanctuary of God or the sacred cultural village is the link between man and his creator from where he gets God's message. Some of the places with sacred cultural villages or sanctuaries of God include; Japan, China, Egypt, Israel, Buganda, Malagasy, Zanzibar, England (London Museum Areas), Rome, Mecca and Greece.

According to God's plan, He administers some places directly. This started during the angelic administration of Kabaka Nnende. Nnende in full is "Nendekerwa obuyinza kulwa Katonda okukulembera" which means that "I have been given powers over heaven and earth to rule on behalf of the Almighty". Nnende was a spiritual angel of God, whom God sent to earth as a judge to deliberate upon the confusion and mayhem. This is when there were many spiritual wars between Satan (Olukokobe) and his angels against angels of God and the messengers of God i.e. prophets. God also sent His angel Kayiuk as the first prophet to liberate the people of earth who were being battered and ill-treated by Satan and his Angel of Death called Walumbe. Angel Nnende warned our forefather Kintu Kitaka Nawansi Kyawadda about the dangers of not having the Sacred Cultural village or Akaalo ka Buganda, or the sanctuary of God, because the society was disorganized. It was full of wars and diseases and Satan and Walumbe were mistreating everybody. As a result the sanctuary of God was set up as Akaalo ka Buganda – The Sacred Cultural Village. This sanctuary is used for worship and prayer where man presents his problems to God. As a result, man overcomes the many problems including war, diseases and ignorance. It is the source of peace, unity and wisdom as God's power is directly manifested to the area. This place was established at Nnono. Buganda should rebuild such a place and save her and generations to come.

Buganda is one of those areas that had the sacred cultural villages or sanctuary of God. Defying the covenant of God is a case before God, because other people would have loved to have this opportunity but they cannot access it. The kingdom gets so many problems and challenges for failure to do this, which was done by many of the former kings. The covenant of God whether written or kept in heritage has to be preserved because it is spiritual. Because of Kintu's obedience, his people were helped to get peace. The disobedience of his twin brother Wasswa Bemba Musota made him lose his seat of power and God's favor. What was Bemba's shrine held by his adorers in commemoration on the banks of river Lubigi on Hoima Road, was also destroyed. There is nothing to show his record like for all other Kings apart from his tyrannical record that continues to face God's wrath by close association of any.

WHAT WENT WRONG WITH AKAALO KA BUGANDA-THE SACRED CULTURAL VILLAGE

Headquarter or sanctuary or base means the origin of man, values and norms of kingship, source of all activities for man, heritage and institution of kingship. This sanctuary of God is at Nnono in Busujju. It is for the entire kingdom of Buganda and for all the blacks. This place is not for mankind or kingship but for God because it represents the covenant of God for us all the blacks and a mirror for all other Kingdoms or States. The spiritual covenant is what God bases on to bless us, to forgive us because it is where God's power descends upon us.

If you defy God's covenant and remain doing wrong, then you are com-mitting a terrible sin. You cannot defy God's covenant and survive His wrath. This has been the beginning of man's downfall, the source of disturbances and war. This is why people are immoral and there is no peace in the country. There is no longer any help from God because God's sanctuary is no longer there or respected or restored. There is no way God can relate with us, to judge our faithfulness to Him and to send us His spirit. Various kings have been practicing this tradition of restoring the sanctuary of God called Akaalo ka Buganda. These are some of them;

• Ssekabaka Kamaanya whose palace was at Kasengejje established it at Kalagala in Bugerere County.
• Ssekabaka Lukanga whose palace was at Mayangayanga established it at Maligita.
•Ssekabaka Nakibinge established it at Ddindo in Kyaggwe.
•Ssekabaka Kimbowa also established it at Ddindo in Kyaggwe.
•Ssekabaka Mwanga Basammuleekkere established it at Kaazi Busaabala in Kyaddondo and this is where it ended.

Ssekabaka Mwanga II was exiled in the Seychelles Island and they in-stalled his youngest son Dawudi Chwa II, who was only two years old! What was the sanctuary of God became a camping site for the scouts and girl guides at Kaazi.

God's convent is forever and stands all the time. The destruction or the criminal neglect for the sanctuary has been the source of moral degeneration and the many problems man is experiencing. The convent that was given to Kintu Kitaka Nnawansi Kyawadda is supposed to be at Nnono as we have already discussed. Transferring it to other places as some kings did was wrong because it was outside God's sanctuary. They could have established it but it was in a wrong position. His grandson Kato Kintu I did not change the position. Others who changed were outside the position of God's favor. This was the beginning of disintegration.

THE SANCTUARY IS THE HERITAGE

The Sanctuary of God was our heritage. It was our convent with God and the museum of all our traditions. This was the institution where we got all the wisdom and understanding. It was a great temple of God, the meeting place for all clan heads where cultural norms and values were stored. All creativity and discoveries were in this place, it was the source of all holiness and indeed our heritage.

People are only interested in accumulating wealth. You cannot get this using God's sanctuary. Those who think they can achieve their selfish ends are only dreaming and are living in imagination. The fortune seekers who want to use it to steal, to sabotage, to be greedy for everything, to break the covenant and accumulate wealth are in a wrong place. They are condemned and heading towards being obliterated to ashes.

Ssekabaka Kateregga got this problem. Ssekabaka Ttembo developed mental illness. Lubendera in the periods before Kato Kintu I dynasty transferred Akaalo ka Buganda and took it to Kkawanga in Busiro County, then he was vaporized, disappeared in the desert where to date after years and years he's heard bellowing. When this happens, they sound the drums to put to silence his occasional mourns. This is the ritual practice for people of those areas as a mark of reminder not to tamper with the sacred village. He came off his throne and has never resurfaced to date, apart from the sounding agonies from his cries. He fought tooth and nail to remove the sanctuary so as to begin his own system but this caused wild fires and floods.

Painting showing Lubendera

The drumming was intended to exorcise his spirit and curses that followed

Ssekabaka Lukanga transferred it to Maligita in Bugerere County and the people in this county were attacked by wild animals, diseases, floods, wild fires and pests. These chased many people out of this county and the place became characterized by the jungle. There is evidence of this up to the present day.

Ssekabaka Ndawula Kyalubimba established it at Bigobyamugenyi in Ssembabule, running away from the many problems that were in Buganda. People in this area were also attacked by diseases, floods, wild fires and pests. These chased many people out of this county and the place became characterized by the jungle, like it was in Bugerere. These sanctuaries were no longer belonging to the state of Buganda but to the kings as individuals because they were established out of positions which did not have God's favor. Akaalo ka Buganda or the Sanctuary lost meaning.

THE ARTISTIC IMPRESSION OF THE KAALO KA BUGANDA

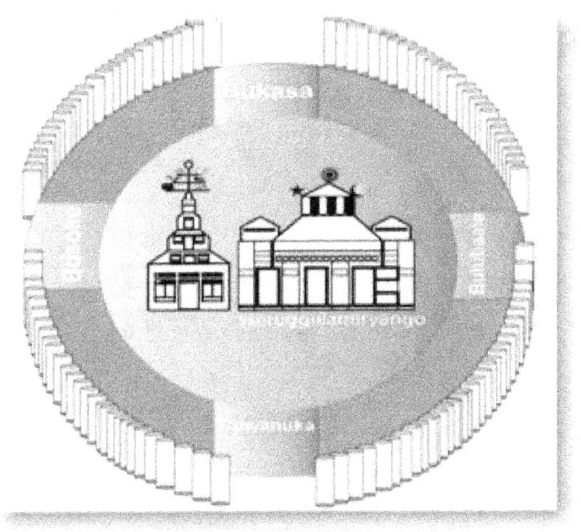

The Sanctuary of God or Akaalo ka Buganda was enclosed in a well knitted reed fence with four major gates or entrances described below:

Buwanuka

This was the main entrance and was meant for prayer and worship and it was the source of God's favor, peace, protection, and good fortune in war and in our clans.

Bukasa

People who used this gate were looking for God's blessing to get children, good families, and good returns in their businesses and occupations. They prayed for good life for their families.

Bulubaale

This gate was used by the spiritual leaders or the priests.

Busoke

People who used this gate had always gone to give thanksgiving, glorifying the name of God and purifying themselves. They wanted to be reminded of God's covenant, wanting to attain knowledge and wisdom.

THE CLAN SYSTEM

Every clan in Buganda has its Headquarter (Obutaka), but at the head-quarters there was a shrine or temple for worshipping for that clan. All the clan shrines had their headquarters at Akaalo ka Buganda. The ad-ministration headquarters for all the clans was the king's palace (Olubiri lwa Kabaka). In the sanctuary there were priests and prophets, and this was their headquarters. At the headquarters of every clan there was a traditional house where training and creativity took place.

This house is used for worship and other things. They communicate with God and to correct all mistakes within the clan. From the beginning, the Baganda were a chosen race and Buganda was God's area. It had the Sanctuary of God Akaalo ka Buganda. That is why there are many songs that have been composed to praise this sanctuary in Luganda.

Akaalo ka Buganda ka dda, akaalo kaaliko nnannyini kko, meaning that this sanctuary is a covenant of God for us generation after generation and it has its guardian. Who is this guardian? This means that the guardian is God. This was a song that was composed to praise God for His mercy.

THE COURTS OF JURISDICTION

Every clan has a headquarter and in the headquarter there was a place known as Embuga or Ekigango (Debating room) or Ekitawuluzi (Court yard) where conflicts within the clan were resolved openly and amicably without resorting to war. In this place trial is by open jury. It was also a meeting place where open discussion used to take place.

THE TOWER OF POWER
(OMULONGOOTI)

There is what we call dual power, Trinity power and earthly power. Dual power comes from the twins i.e. the divine power and the earthly power referred to as Abalongo (i.e. live and neutral wire). The dual power links people to God; this twin is loosely referred to as Entolontozi (meteorite) who is always rested on top of a tower to work as an antenna. It is because of this twin that the tower is referred to as Omulongooti (tower) which comes from Omulongo, meaning twin power. It is erected and long in height symbolizing that God is up in heaven. It symbolizes the praise of God who is above everything. The tower is built in form of a flat house with two floors.

A person is free to raise his prayers in isolation of other people and he is free to give thanks giving in a loud prayer. These prayers are instantly answered by God.

THE MAIN TEMPLE

The main and high temple is referred to as Sseruggulamiryango (House of worship with many doors) and it is the cathedral for all the small temples or shrines built for purposes of worshiping God. This cathedral or Sseruggulamiryango has nine doors representing the nine doors of heaven. In Sseruggulamiryango people pray to God to sanctify them. They pray for peace, good life, and fortune in businesses, good families, fair administration, protection and accumulation of wealth. It was a huge cathedral.

HOUSE OF THE TRINITY

The trinity is composed of Musoke, Mukasa and Kiwanuka. However, this house is headed by the spirit of the highest God called Mwoyo Kitiibwa i.e. Holy Spirit of God the Almighty. He guides the world from where it is coming from and guides about where it is heading to. This in Buganda is referred to as obuvo (the beginning), obugendo (the journey) n'obuddo (the end); which is the source of knowing what is right and what is wrong. The Spirit knows your life right from birth to death. This is God's heaven and earth. This spirit of the most high God lives in all living creatures and gives them knowledge and understanding. This is the trinity and this house is their area of operation.

THE ROYAL FIRE IN THE SANCTUARY

Every sanctuary of God has the basic characteristic and this is praise and worship. Fire is a symbol of God's power and for His heavenly king-dom.

This is why people make fire as He commanded while in prayer. In Akaalo ka Buganda or the sanctuary of God there is this royal fire (Ekyoto) where they make fire and adding spices, perfumes and anointing oils (obuloosa n'obubaani). This is why the Baganda say Kyaka wano, Kyaka Zulu, Kyaka Tanzania which means it is burning ablaze. This means burning fire. Every shrine has this fire made in a place called ekyoto in Buganda. There are even many names of people related to fire or fire making such as Omukumamu (Fire maker), Ssemanda (Burning char-coal), Omuseesa (the one who adds more firewood to the fire), Kiriro (Fire), Mmanda (charcoal) and Kinyata (burning ashes).

Fire represents the power of God. On the firesides, we present to God our requests because everything belongs to Him including firing us up.

THE ROYAL DRUMS
(MAWUUNO)

The drums are the rhythms that give us loud voices of praise. The loud voice raised to God is called Musisi, Kagugumuko or the rhythm that sets in God's pulse similar to the earthquakes. The sticks used to beat the drums are called eminyolo which comes from the verb okunyolwa, meaning something that takes away all worries. It is also called omubala, meaning to count, which further means that as people praise God they count their blessings.

The drum is used even in other functions of celebration (embaga) and rituals of Buganda like on weddings, because on every function where drums are sounded, people count their blessings. This is one way in which we fulfill God's covenant because it is one of his requirements for us to praise His name as our creator. The drum is used to summon others including the spirits. It can also be used when relaying information you want to give to others. In the sanctuary this drum is called Mawuuno or Kalyabugalula or Kalyabugatte i.e. call or worship gatherer.

THE MUESEUM

All states have these institutions where they keep records and archives where information about great men, warriors, men of achievements is kept. Akaalo ka Buganda had an archive. It is in this place where all Buganda's history about warriors, great kings, creativity, great scientists was kept. This helped to bring about healthy competition and hard work among the Baganda, stimulating innovation and peaceful development.

THE HOSPITAL AND A TRADITIONAL PHARMACY

In the Scared Cultural Village or Akaalo ka Buganda there was a hospital which had great doctors and scientists who were skilled in the treatment of various diseases, preventable and non-preventable. It also had a pharmacy that was used in research about various diseases. These two institutions worked hand in hand.

THE RULING COUNCIL SECRETARIATES

In the Sacred Cultural Village or Akaalo ka Buganda, existed the ruling council secretariats. This was known as ebitongole by'Abakungu or the secretariat within Akaalo ka Buganda and the clan heads used it as a base to perform many kingdom duties. Many came to this place for consultations on issues that required wise counsel so as to serve the kingdom better. In other words, they used to come for administration and service delivery.

THE TRAINING SCHOOL OR COLLEGE

This was the traditional place in Akaalo ka Buganda or sanctuary of God where training of people in various skills was carried out. For example training of priests, sanctification of people, and where people were equipped with skills necessary for society transformation. It was for retooling in skills. Therefore, in Akaalo ka Buganda many things took place. Whenever somebody said that he was going to Buganda, it meant that he was going to Akaalo ka Buganda because it had all aspects of civilization and knowledge. The basis was in national interest and the covenant between society and God.

THE SEAT OF THE HEAVENLY KINGDOM

All creatures are in link with God the almighty.
God created the entire universe and its fullness.
God uses His creation as He wishes to co-create and have creatures multiply.
Man survives on other creatures that were created by God or by enjoying the fruits of God's creation.

God saw that everything He created was good and named all creatures.
The world has operated on these principles all the time.

Man looks at the God's creation and the names given to creatures and appreciates the wonders of His work in the entire environment. This is the heritage. That is why people on many occasions consult the tradition-al doctors or healers, priests and prophets who have spiritual powers to discover more about God's heritage in the things that they use like the herbs, the rituals they perform, the forecasting and prophecy they give, the words they say, language, morals, cure of diseases, what they use to prevent bad situations, to treat diseases and to accumulate wealth or how to become rich.

Waking up from sleep is like a television remote or radio broadcast. Who knows how to operate a remote? The best example is that of the dry cells. They are called dry cells because they have powerful cells in them that give them power to operate and to make bulbs create light. This power comes from the Kiwanuka spirit which relates to fire that he controls. This electric shock is the power of God's creation. This power combines to make positive and negative charge and thereafter make light.

A person has to get knowledge of God the Creator so as to understand His creation.

God's creation helps him to understand his culture and heritage.

His culture enables him to understand God's covenant.

Then from this covenant he understands the norms.

The norms make him to know the values and acceptable behavior.

The acceptable behaviors and values enable him understand where he is coming from and where he is going.

What God is doing in one's life, what He will do or what He did, makes Him a perfect God. This is God's heritage for man.

WHAT DO SO AS TO GUARD AGAINST OR TO AVOID PAST MISTAKES?

What people should guard against is doing things people of good morals are not supposed to do. People should avoid doing those things which do not please God and doing only those that please God. You should avoid behaving like animals. This is a terrible sin. Eating stuff that is not sup-posed to be eaten by man is also a terrible sin. Changing your form is defying God's creation, telling lies; hypocrisy, maundering and things of that kind are terrible sins.

THE DONTS TO OBSERVE IN AKAALO KA BUGANDA

People should use the right entrances and exits. People should avoid sexual immorality in The Akaalo ka Buganda because it is a holy place. They should avoid acts of human sacrifice in the holy places. People should avoid murder of any kind or else they risk being judged in the strongest sense. They should always be fair while making judgment.

AKAALO KA BUGANDA IS SO AMAZING
A PLACE OF MANY WONDERS

The world was created on a series of foundations given its heritage and given channels of communication, several languages, different dimensions, understanding, economic institutions, norms and cultures and several types of food stuffs that are different. Leadership of different states is therefore supposed to follow the foundations on which God created them. The leadership was required to follow the plan of God. When this is not followed, the people in the world are not to blame for their life styles.

This is a clear indication that Buganda is a special country before God and the Baganda are a chosen race. This is why its heritage vested in the sacred cultural village Akaalo ka Buganda is supposed to be treated and preserved with keen interest to save the people from suffering. God has a grand plan for every race. The Baganda demonstrate in their belief sys-tem and crafts-manship that they are naturally gifted. It is in the way they were created and as they are influenced by the environment around them. That is why God put in place life mechanisms, some of which are clearly known and those that are still hidden.

God sending his messengers and prophets to save his people is not a new thing. However, people know their heritages and cultures and they preserve it at all costs. They stick to their life mechanisms. You cannot change them. They may not abandon their belief system. These cultures and traditions constitute God's covenant with the people and they know this is His plan for them. This explains why God separated us in colour, races, languages, names, understanding, feeding habits, crops grown, leadership, ways of life, worship, the way we treat diseases, dress code and many aspects of life. They struggle to preserve them at all costs.

Therefore, it is not good to defy God's plan and His covenant with mankind. It is very dangerous to copy and add other things from outside because you have copied from other regions or you have read about them in books trusting your personal knowledge or experience. This is equivalent to disobedience to God and despising His holy name.

Finally brothers and sisters, I am requesting you to do the right thing that suit your traditions and what pleases God. Avoid the ungodly practices. The truth is that The Sanctuary of God is very important; it is the link between us and God. Our cultural heritages that were agreed upon at Nnono are our covenant with Him. It is dangerous to mix it with other values from outside. People will support you as you copy things from other areas. People will never respect you for that because for them they know the truth. This is why a person or a priest who is a native but belongs to another denomination and belief, is not ashamed to serve or fulfill duties in his native denomination and also as a mark, pay homage to the Kabaka or his tradition leader and thus takes him as his master. If you defy the cultures, norms and traditions, you will become a failure and many people will desert you. In a very short time, you may face God's judgment and punishment. You will be convicted and found guilty of doing things contrary to God's plan.

SUMMARY

For so long, the world has been submerged in myths and confusion of the numerous religious teachings, subjects and interpretations. In this book, we demystify all myths and clarify on all confusions by answering all the unanswered questions and setting the facts right. This book is a starting point for the world to make correct interpretations without personal bias, tribalism or religious affiliation; rather every interpretation should be based on the truth. The content in this book was carefully derived un-der spiritual guidance by God upon the writers thereby giving it all the authenticity to be Divine, and hence God's word.

Thank you.